IN A SHAKER KITCHEN

IN A
SHAKER KITCHEN

100 TRADITIONAL AMERICAN RECIPES

NORMA MACMILLAN

PAVILION

First published in Great Britain in 1995 by
PAVILION BOOKS LIMITED
26 Upper Ground, London SE1 9PD

Text and recipes copyright © 1995 by Norma MacMillan
The moral right of the author has been asserted

Food styling and photographs © 1995 by Philip Webb
All other photographs, see page 152
Home Economist: Jane Stevenson

Designed by Bernard Higton

A CIP catalogue record for this book is available from the British Library

ISBN 185793 578 0

Printed and bound in Spain by Cayfosa

2 4 6 8 10 9 7 5 3 1

This book may be ordered by post direct from the publisher.
Please contact the Marketing Department. But try your bookshop first.

CONTENTS

INTRODUCTION

> *Put your hands to work and your hearts to God, and benefits will befall thee.*
>
> Mother Ann Lee

It is over two hundred years since the founding of Shakerism in the United States. At its peak, in the middle of the last century, the United Society of Believers in Christ's Second Appearing had nearly 6000 members, living in 18 prosperous communities that stretched from New England to Ohio and Kentucky. Today, numbers have dwindled to a handful, in one community in Maine, but the treasured principles of unity and simplicity still live on, as does the legacy of the Shaker cooks who laboured with love and dedication to feed their Brothers and Sisters.

The Shaker movement began in Manchester, England, in the middle of the eighteenth century, with a group of Quakers who had been influenced by the radical and apocalyptical teachings of French Calvinists known as the French Prophets or Camisards. Meetings would begin in silent meditation, but then the worshippers would fall into trances and start to tremble or shake, shout or sing, and move about uncontrollably when they felt filled with the presence of the Holy Spirit. Because of this, they came to be called 'Shaking Quakers' or Shakers.

Ann Lee (then named Lees), the illiterate 22-year-old daughter of a blacksmith, joined the sect in 1758. Four years later she married, and had four

SHAKER SISTERS AT ELIJAH WILD'S HOUSE, WHICH WAS THE FIRST TO BE BUILT AT SHIRLEY

children in quick succession, all of whom died in infancy. Her reaction to these tragedies was to become convinced that sex and marriage were the source of all evil in the world – violence, greed, disease, famine, poverty and all other forms of human misery – and that only by men and women remaining celibate all their lives, relating to each other innocently as brother and sister, and confessing their sins, could salvation be achieved. The other members of the sect came to share her views, and eventually she became the leader.

The Shakers were regarded with suspicion, even fear, because of their criticisms of the established church and even more because of the religious ecstasy of their worship. Ann Lee was accused of blasphemy and imprisoned, an experience that had a profound effect. Upon her release she told her followers that she had had a revelation while in prison, and that the spirit of Christ had come upon her.

Her powerful conviction was that she was to be God's instrument to found a new and more perfect society on earth. She took the title of 'Mother of the New Creation', and declared that she had had a vision of a chosen people awaiting her in the New World. So in 1774 eight members of the United Society of Believers in Christ's Second Appearing, as the Shakers formally called themselves, including Mother Ann Lee and her husband, set sail from England.

This small group of Believers arrived in New York at the outbreak of the American Revolution. The first communal home, at Watervliet (then called Niskeyuna), New York, was built in the wilderness, and the new settlers had to work hard to sustain their bodies and their spirits. As in England, they were persecuted for their religious beliefs and practices as well as being regarded as English spies. Some colonists accused them of treason because they wouldn't take up arms in the War of Independence.

Mother Ann travelled and preached, hoping to inspire new converts, and the number of Believers grew. But the energy this required left her exhausted, and she died in 1784, aged 48.

At this time, the celibate Shakers, both individuals and families, lived separately, gathering on Sunday to worship. It was Mother Ann's successors, Joseph Meacham and Lucy Wright, who created the framework of communal settlements of Shaker 'Families' that shared all work and possessions, with the aim of becoming self-sufficient. It began with all the Shakers in a vicinity assembling at the farm of one member, and selling all other landholdings. To the Shakers, this act represented a kind of separation from 'the World', which is what they called non-Believers. The first community was formed at New Lebanon, New York in 1787, and by 1794 eleven communities had been established in New York and New England.

Before the dwellings and farm buildings were enlarged, this usually meant many heads crowded under the same roof. But because the Shakers were excellent farmers and worked hard, communities eventually spread over very large tracts of land, comprising pastures with flocks of sheep and cows, fields of maize and other grains, orchards of fruit and nut trees, woodlands, meadows, lakes and springs, acres of kitchen gardens full of vegetables and herbs, cow barns, hen houses, dairies, workshops, dwellings and meeting houses.

> *Do all your work as though you had a thousand years to live, and as you would if you knew you must die tomorrow.*
>
> MOTHER ANN LEE

In addition to the realization of the principle of communal property, Joseph Meacham and Lucy Wright established a structure of Shaker leadership. A hierarchy of elders and eldresses, deacons and deaconesses, and trustees – both men and women sharing equally in religious responsibilities – governed each Family, and a central ministry oversaw the community. The Shaker 'capital' was at New Lebanon.

The Covenant, first drawn up at this time and revised over several years, can be seen as a kind of Shaker Constitution. In it the system of commitment to Shakerism was set out. Prospective converts could enter a 'novitiate', to see if the Shaker lifestyle suited them. Once committed they gave up all their personal possessions, and whatever trade they had practised in the World for profit – as blacksmiths, cobblers, tailors, weavers, bookbinders, farmers and so on – was henceforth to be worked at for the good of the community. Signing the Covenant was meant to be a lifetime commitment, but it wasn't irrevocable: if a member wanted to leave, he was free to go.

The well-ordered framework of Shaker life was governed by rules or 'Millenial Laws' that prescribed separation of the sexes, plainness and

ELDER HENRY BLINN AND HIS BEE HIVES, CANTERBURY SHAKER VILLAGE

neatness of dress, proper behaviour, diet, education of young people, a complex system of job rotation, colours of paint for buildings, simplicity and absence of all adornment, set times for rising and eating, and so on. These rules were observed in all the communities, which made them very alike despite the miles between them. With every aspect of life regulated, the Shakers were almost completely removed from worldly cares and pressures. Their lives were calm and peaceful, with their rites of worship being the opportunity to raise their voices and dance in praise of the Lord.

There were normally several Families in each community, and as communities grew and flourished, each Family could number as many as 150

Brethren and Sisters, although 50–100 was more common. Each Family lived together in its own dwelling, with men and women strictly segregated except at meals or in supervised meetings, and had its own fields, orchards and kitchen gardens. Members of different Families were not encouraged to fraternize, but came together for services and funerals and helped each other when required, particularly in business ventures.

The much-derided shaking, whirling and jumping that characterized the worship of the early Believers was changed by Joseph Meacham, to institute a more orderly service. Men and women sat on opposite sides of the room. Simple dances were performed in unison, the most common being stepping forwards and back in a kind of march. Lively hymns were sung unaccompanied (over time, 10,000 songs were written, some original and some with words put to tunes 'redeemed' from the World).

Mother Ann had prophesied that there would be a second Shaker revival in the West, so at the beginning of the nineteenth century missionaries were sent out to the developing frontier. Over the next 20 years, nine new communities were established, in Ohio, Indiana and Kentucky as well as in New York.

By the 1820s a more corporate type of order had replaced the early, essentially communistic sharing of possessions and work. Shaker communities became very prosperous, due to their efficient production of goods that the World wanted and needed – dried medicinal and culinary herbs, garden seeds, fresh fruits and vegetables, maple syrup and sugar, preserves and fruit wines, eggs and cheese, handcrafted items such as brooms, straw hats and wooden boxes, and cattle in the western communities. Shaker-prepared goods, made with care from the best

> *They have an extensive orchard, containing a great variety of excellent fruit, large medical and seed gardens, which are in fine order. These gardens are very profitable, as their herbs and seeds are every where sought after and purchased, being always esteemed better than any other which can be procured. They take great pains in drying and packing their medical herbs, and so highly are they valued that they have frequent orders for them from Europe to a very large amount.*
>
> FROM *PECULIARITIES OF THE SHAKERS*, 1832

raw materials, had an excellent reputation, and the Believers had the added advantage of marketing their own products.

The Shakers enjoyed a quality of life that was better than most Americans could aspire to at the time. Even their animals were kept in spotlessly clean and pleasant conditions. However, the Believers still observed the basic tenets of simplicity and frugality and eschewed anything that was not useful (new technology, though, was embraced and even improved on). Food was one of their few indulgences, although the Millenial Laws of 1821 reminded members that they should be content with a 'common' diet, and should not ask for anything special unless they were unwell.

Prospective members came to join the communities, attracted by the generous table and cleanliness and order of Shaker communities. (This caused tensions as older Believers thought only converts with sincere religious conviction should be accepted.) There were also 'winter Shakers' who arrived at the onset of cold weather, stayed to partake of the plain but delicious fare, and other comforts, and then left in the spring when the hard work began again.

There are no high cloister walls around their buildings, and no dark courts lead to their dwellings; but God's bright sunlight is invited everywhere, to cheer with its rays, this simple and unassuming people. The visitor or traveler will not find the forbidding words, "No admittance," written on any of their gates or doors, but meets with a kind and hearty welcome, with an invitation to examine and judge for himself; while hardly a day passes by in which hundreds of strangers do not come through their farms and villages.

FROM THE SHAKER, DECEMBER, 1871

The Believers welcomed travellers and visitors and served them bountiful meals, as well as offering overnight accommodation and Shaker-made goods to buy. One sophisticated visitor to the Hancock, Massachusetts community in the 1830s wrote that his meals were 'worthy of Delmonico's'. Other visitors, many of them famous, were not so complimentary. Charles Dickens spent a day at Mount Lebanon in June 1842, and his first impressions used the word 'grim' seven times. Other writers, such as Hawthorne and Melville, were also disparaging, and Shakers were satirized in popular magazines.

> *Only a part of the Shaker people eat any meat at all. Many use no food produced by animals, denying themselves even milk, butter, and eggs. At Mount Lebanon, and in some of the other societies, two tables are set, one with, the other without meat. They consume much fruit, eating it at every meal.*
>
> Charles Nordhoff
> Communistic Societies of the United States, 1875

Even those who praised the Shakers for their industry found their religious practices bizarre and worthy of ridicule and their rules to be very harsh. Without doubt, though, the World was fascinated by the Shakers.

Material prosperity began to cause internal tensions amongst the Believers, with many, particularly the young, becoming impatient with strict rules in the midst of worldly temptations. Membership began to decline. Possibly as a reaction to this, in 1837 a revival of spiritual manifestions began, with Believers falling into trances, shaking and whirling as they did in the beginning, and receiving inspirational and prophetic messages from Mother Ann as well as the Apostles, the Angel Gabriel, historical figures such as Napoleon and George Washington, and Native American spirit guides. These strange occurrences quickly spread through all the communities, and carried on for a decade.

In the United States, outside of these communities, the early and middle years of the nineteenth century was a period of great change and upheaval, as the population almost doubled, there was a mass movement westwards, and the country became industrialized and more urbanized. Food was abundant, particularly meat, and spirits were cheap and plentiful. So much eating and drinking caused a malaise termed dyspepsia, for which quacks offered all manner of cures. The temperance movement, which was then gaining momentum, wanted to reform the national diet too, to make it more healthy.

The Shakers shared these concerns, and many articles in their publications advocated a plain but wholesome diet containing plenty of fruits and

IN THE SHAKER VILLAGES, BUILDINGS WERE PAINTED DIFFERENT COLOURS ACCORDING TO THEIR FUNCTION. WHITE WAS EXPENSIVE AND WAS THEREFORE RESERVED FOR SPIRITUAL BUILDINGS

Bread is called the 'staff of life.' Its importance in dieting cannot be over-estimated. The bread of a people determines largely the character of that people...Is the American superfine bolted flour the primary cause of national dyspepsia, and also of the loss of teeth?...After the wheat (which of all food contains all the properties, and in the proportions, of the component elements of the body) has been 'killed' in grinding, these elements are separated, and some of the most essential are thrown away entirely; the remainder is made into enervating, constipating, dyspepsia-creating, superfine white bread...

FROM *SHAKER AND SHAKERESS*, NOVEMBER, 1873

vegetables and whole-grain bread, eaten in moderation when hungry. For ten years (from 1837–1847), there was a ban on meat in Shaker communities, and rules were instituted against alcohol, tea and coffee. Not all Believers were in favour of vegetarianism, so in most communities there were tables for those on a 'regular' diet and tables for those who preferred a 'bloodless' diet. Temperance, too, was not strictly enforced, and by the end of the 1850s tea and coffee were again being drunk.

At this time, thousands of Americans joined religious movements that offered alternative lifestyles, including the Society of Believers. Most Shaker converts were evangelical Christians, but some were non-Christians who believed in the principle of a communistic society, while others were less spiritual Christians who were attracted to the secure and comfortable lifestyle. Charles Nordhoff, an American journalist who studied all the 'communistic societies' in the United States at the time, including the Shakers, the Oneida Perfectionists and the Amana Society, gives a not uncritical account of the Shaker way of life then. He noted that Believers demanded hard work of their members, that some communities were more prosperous than others, and that members within Families could be from very different backgrounds. He also wrote: 'In practical life they are industrious, peaceful, honest, highly ingenious, patient of toil, and extraordinarily cleanly.' But '...they do not pretend that their celibate life is without hardships or difficulties.'

After the Civil War, the population in Shaker communities continued to decline, due largely to the increase in employment opportunities for men and the lure of the West. Initially, the Believers tried to keep up their numbers by adopting orphans and taking in poor children (many of whom left when they were old enough), but orphanages began to be established and living conditions were improving for the poor. As the general standard of living improved all over the United States, the unworldly and celibate Shaker way of life was no longer such an appealing option.

To attract new members, it was decided to relax some of the stricter rules, to allow music and reading as well as the planting of flower gardens. Attention was drawn to the sexual equality in Shaker life, to appeal to women who at that time had few rights to property and independence (although, in fact, the only true equality was in the Shaker religious leadership). Worship was changed, to more closely resemble a Protestant church service, with no marching. Non-uniform dress was allowed as the twentieth century began, and the lifestyle became more like that in the World. More women than men signed the Covenant, and Shaker societies became increasingly feminized. The result was a reduced workforce, which meant that labour had to be hired and supplies bought in. Many of the once prosperous Shaker businesses could not compete with factory-produced goods and cheaper prices.

A GROUP OF SISTERS IN TYPICAL SHAKER CLOTHING

As at the beginning, the groups of Believers, mainly ageing Sisters, gradually gathered together, relocating to fewer and smaller communities and selling off furniture and land no longer worked. A once very prosperous national organization had shrunk to three small Families in New England, comprising 50 or so Believers, by 1947.

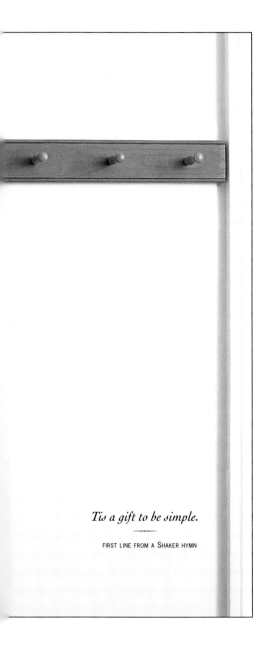

Tis a gift to be simple.

FIRST LINE FROM A SHAKER HYMN

In the 1950s and 60s, as the United States became increasingly affluent, a renaissance of interest in the Shakers began, helped along by a general religious revival. The rural Shaker communities seemed to offer a haven of peace in an ever more commercial world that was full of turmoil. Antique collectors and dealers became very interested in Shaker furniture; Shaker manuscripts and diaries were sought by libraries; composers such as Aaron Copland borrowed Shaker songs for their compositions. Devoted supporters bought and restored former Shaker communities as museum villages.

In 1959 Eldress Emma B King of Canterbury, New Hampshire, established a trust fund with resources from the sale of Shaker lands and assets, to provide for the remaining Believers as well as to preserve the Shaker heritage. In 1965, with only two communities of Shaker Sisters still in existence, she declared the membership rolls closed to new converts. However, Believers living at the other Shaker community, at Sabbathday Lake, Maine, were not in agreement with this, and the conflict caused the two groups to split. Today, in 1994, there are no longer any Shakers at Canterbury, but the community at Sabbathday Lake lives on, with eight members – two men and six women between the ages of 30 and 90.

Shakerism has changed with the times: Sisters no longer wear plain ankle-length dresses and bonnets, and Brothers cotton trousers and straw hats; they use computers and watch television; they take vacations and fly in airplanes. But they still aspire to unity and simplicity, produce goods that enjoy the same excellent reputation as their predecessors' did, and worship God in song-filled services. New converts are not sought, but there are about 50 enquiries each year about membership. As Sister Frances Carr said recently: 'I don't think that God, who is in charge of it all, will let Shakerism simply come to an end. But at this point, I couldn't give you a clue as to how He or She will do it.'

Shaker communities were always orderly and clean, with buildings and furniture constructed from local materials. Good ventilation and light were deemed essential, so buildings had many windows; floors were polished but not covered by rugs; walls of storage cupboards and drawers prevented there being any clutter. All was finished simply and unadorned, made solely to fulfil a function, as the Millenial Laws dictated, yet one imagines that the Shakers would have derived satisfaction from their good work even if they could not always admit its beauty.

The Shakers aspired to be self-sufficient, but unlike the Amish, the Believers didn't eschew new technology. They were keen to try out every new invention, from indoor plumbing and electricity to telephones and cars, and they were always designing devices or improving on those they bought, to lighten their labours and save time. They used the most up-to-date farm machinery, and were pioneers in the safe bottling of fruits and vegetables. Among the inventions credited to them are an improved wood-burning stove, a washing machine, a means of making false teeth, a hernia truss, the first circular saw in the United States, a revolving oven, a dough-kneading machine, a water-powered butter churn, a 'self-acting' cheese press, a mechanical apple peeler, a pea sheller and a fly trap.

Since the time that the Believers first offered their hand-crafted goods for sale, the World has coveted them. Nineteenth-century visitors to Shaker communities took away freshly baked pies, jams, apple butter and applesauce, dried fruits, cucumber pickles, cured meats, fruit wines and cordials, honey, maple syrup and sugar, eggs, cheese, butter, and fresh

fruits and vegetables. Shaker merchants travelled far and wide selling brooms, straw hats and bonnets, jeans, wooden boxes, dried herbs and garden seeds. Today, genuine Shaker-made items fetch astronomic prices at auction, and reproduction or 'Shaker-inspired' furniture and objects – including peg rails, multi-drawered cabinets and cupboards, and kitchen units – are very fashionable.

The Shaker Seed wagon was a welcome sight in the last century. The Brethren had an excellent reputation as shrewd but fair traders who were honest in the advertising of their goods. The Shaker seed business began small, with the seedsmen selling locally, but it became a huge and very profitable industry. In many of the communities, whole fields were given over to raising vegetable seeds, and the Brethren experimented with hybridizing to produce new and better varieties.

Once the seeds were manually harvested and cleaned, they were packed into hand-folded and -sealed paper packets, which gave the cultivation instructions. (This was the first time seeds were put up in small paper envelopes in the United States.) At first the neat and colourful packets were printed by hand, but later presses were devised for printing them as well as 'machines' for filling them. As the business expanded, seed catalogues were also printed, giving 'recipes for cookery' together with the lists of available varieties. One list included six varieties of beans, six

> *Time lost can never be regained. After allowing yourself proper time for rest, don't live a single hour of your life without doing exactly what is to be done in it, and going straight through it from beginning to end. Work, play, study, whatever it is, take hold at once and finish it up squarely and clearly; then to the next thing, without letting any moments drop out between.*
>
> FROM *SHAKER AND SHAKERESS*, JUNE, 1874

The following seeds are selected with peculiar care, being the choicest kinds of the different varieties; and as such they will recommend themselves. They will be sold on the most reasonable terms by the pound, or put up in small papers for retailing, to suit the convenience of customers.

FROM *A CATALOGUE OF GARDEN SEEDS RAISED BY THE UNITED SOCIETY OF SHAKERS, MOUNT LEBANON, COLUMBIA COUNTY, NEW YORK*

varieties of beetroot, five varieties of cabbage, six varieties of lettuce, three varieties of melon, five varieties of radish, plus aubergine, asparagus, salsify, 'spinage', sea kale, sweet pepper, sage, summer savory, nasturtium and two varieties of parsley.

Growing, drying and selling medicinal and culinary herbs was another lucrative industry for most of the Shaker communities. In the late eighteenth and early nineteenth centuries, herbal remedies were widely used, and Shaker-made distillations, ointments, powders, herbal teas and other medicaments were in demand. They shipped medicinal herbs all over the United States as well as abroad, to Europe, Australia and even India (they are considered to have been the first to market medicinal herbs and herbal medicines on a commercial scale). Initially, wild herbs, roots, barks and flowers were gathered and sold; eventually thousands of varieties were cultivated in the extensive herb gardens.

Shaker Sisters used fresh herbs liberally in their cooking, noting that herbs turn even the simplest dish into 'a fascinating, outstanding viand'. They passed on that advice to the cooks in the World, in the leaflets that accompanied dried culinary herbs.

As with so many other Shaker industries, stiff competition from the industrialized world proved to be too great. But in the 1970s the herb business was revived at Sabbathday Lake, and herbs are sold today in their shop and through mail order.

A POSTER ADVERTISING SHAKER SEEDS. THE SHAKERS SHUNNED ORNAMENT IN THEIR OWN LIVES
BUT IN THE NAME OF GOOD BUSINESS WERE PREPARED TO USE STYLISH DESIGN

In the nineteenth century, life for the Believers meant hard work, whether in the fields, the workshops, the dairy or kitchen. All were industrious, unless they were ill, and each person had his or her appointed task. A set schedule ordered their lives, with the ringing of bells: all rose at the same time, gathered for breakfast at 6 am, started and finished work at the same time, had dinner at noon and supper at 6 pm, and went to bed at the same time. They were admonished to be considerate of others, to be quiet in their speech and movements, and to take great care with their personal cleanliness.

The Brothers and Sisters of a Family lived in the same dwelling, but in separate quarters and often with separate stairs and doors so they would not have any private contact. Men and women ate in separate shifts or at separate tables.

Although the Shakers professed to believe that women should have equal rights in society – and they invested God with both masculine and feminine attributes – all work was divided on traditional gender lines: women worked indoors at cooking, cleaning, sewing, ironing, spinning and weaving cloth as well as tending to the hen houses and dairies and filling the herb and seed packets; while men did more varied work in the fields and shops as well as travelling to sell Shaker-made goods. Of course, sharing the tasks would have brought men and women together, which might have led to irresistible temptation, and all work was seen as equal in God's eyes. But, as Lawrence Foster notes, in *Women, Family and Utopia*, visitors to Shaker communities often commented that the women appeared sallow in complexion and less happy than the men. However, there is little evidence in Shaker journals and diaries that anyone objected to the traditional roles.

A system of job rotation was followed, with each Believer, male or female, serving a set time at a task before moving on to another one. If an individual was very productive at a particular task, he or she remained there, and deacons and deaconesses stayed in their supervisory positions. Shaker Sisters served monthly 'turns' in the kitchen, then moved on to the dairy or wash house; tours were also served in the weaving shop and herb house. Seasonal activities such as maple-sugaring or fruit bottling brought all the Sisters together.

In the large kitchens, the Sisters worked in teams of two or three. Young girls served a kind of apprenticeship in the kitchens, helping the Sisters to prepare the tremendous amount of food that was required to feed the Family each day, as well as visitors and hired help. The kitchens were run efficiently, with each Sister having specific duties under the supervision of the deaconess who issued the instructions and doled out the supplies.

All was spotlessly clean, with whitewashed walls, well-scrubbed wooden tables and shining polished pots and pans. There was efficient built-in storage for everything, and many kitchen utensils were fashioned of wood from locally grown trees: measures, scoops, bowls, mortars and pestles, and the familiar oval boxes that were used to hold everything except liquids. Enormous iron kettles, hung on arched, swing-away brackets, were kept full of simmering soups and stews all through the day, and huge ovens never cooled with the baking of so many pies and loaves of bread.

This hive of industry and activity, with its warmth and enticing aromas, must have been a favourite place to work. Certainly it drew in other Sisters and Brethren, because one of the Millenial Laws forbids anyone 'to throng the kitchen or to go into it unnecessarily while the cooks are employed in it'.

The Sisters who prepared the food also served it. The Believers gathered quietly in the dining hall, at the long bare trestle tables set with plain white dishes. After kneeling for a silent grace they ate quickly, in silence, speaking only in a whisper if they wanted something. One Sister might read aloud: extracts from the previous day's newspaper, reports from other Shaker communities or a short story.

Each group of four people, or 'square', had its own servings of food and condiments. All could eat as much as wanted to satisfy the appetite, but if

> *You will perceive that everything here is conducted systematically; the meals, labor, worship, recreation and sleep, all succeed in such regular order, that one thing never interferes with another. Consequently, the members all acting together in concert, and all endeavoring to promote each other's happiness, perform a great amount of labor, without any individual appearing to make very great exertion...*
>
> FROM *PECULIARITIES OF THE SHAKERS*, 1832

you took something on to your plate you finished it (except for bones and inedible skins). Nothing was to be wasted – you 'Shakered' your plate.

Early Shaker cooking was very plain and frugal fare, but as the communities prospered, food became plentiful and varied. Meals were simple but wholesome and delicious, made from the freshest fruits and vegetables in season or home-bottled produce, rich cream and butter from the dairy, home-reared meat and freshly caught fish, eggs from the hen house, breads of all kinds leavened with yeast from home-grown hops, and herbs gathered that morning from the gardens. As noted by a Sister Marcia in *Good House-keeping* magazine in 1905: 'On the ordinary farm the choicest of everything goes to market, while in a Shaker Village the vegetables, cream, meats, etc. are used at home.'

The kitchen Sisters were thrifty and inventive and were always looking for new ideas and inspiration. Just as with cooks in the World, they clipped recipes from magazines and newspapers, and wrote them by hand in their journals. They shared them with their fellow Sisters too. The monthly periodical of the Society of Believers, published between 1871 and 1899 (first called *The Shaker* and later *Shaker and Shakeress*, *The Shaker Manifesto* and, finally, *The Manifesto*), included many recipes and household hints as well as articles from correspondents on food and healthy eating. There were also recipes in a series of almanacs printed from 1882 to 1884.

Shaker recipes usually gave precise weights and measures, although these were sometimes unusual: 'butter the size of a horse chestnut' or enough

A MODERN INTERPRETATION OF A SHAKER KITCHEN

cream to fill a particular bowl. Other recipes might be just lists of ingredients without directions.

In 1882 *Mary Whitcher's Shaker House-Keeper* appeared, the only Shaker cookery book published in the nineteenth century. It contained 150 recipes, plus menus for each day of the week. The book advertised medicines, especially the merits of the sarsaparilla syrup produced by the Canterbury Shakers, and was given away.

❧

This is a collection of recipes inspired by the cooking of the Shakers in the last century. The skills and achievements of the kitchen Sisters represent the best of American country cooking: plain and simple fare that is wholesome and natural, seasonal and abundant, but above all delicious. Methods used in this book are modern; now unfashionable ingredients have been replaced; and quantities of butter and cream have been reduced. But the old-fashioned virtues embodied by the Shaker kitchen will always remain.

A FEW NOTES ON INGREDIENTS AND MEASUREMENTS

For the best results, use only the freshest ingredients, produced as naturally as possible: eggs from free-range chickens, sweet unsalted butter, real maple syrup, pure vanilla essence, pressed apple juice and fresh herbs (dried can be substituted in most cases; use one-third the quantity given).

Two sets of measures have been given in all the recipes: metric and imperial. Follow just one set when preparing a recipe as the two are not exact equivalents. Spoon measures (1 tsp = 5 ml, 1 tbsp = 15 ml) are level.

Recipes have been tested using size-3 eggs. All baking was done in a conventional, not fan-assisted, oven. A mixture of plain and strong plain flours, or self-raising flour, is used to approximate the result obtained with American flour.

> *All meals should be eaten calmly and deliberately and as pleasantly as possible.*
>
> FROM *THE MANIFESTO*, NOVEMBER, 1880

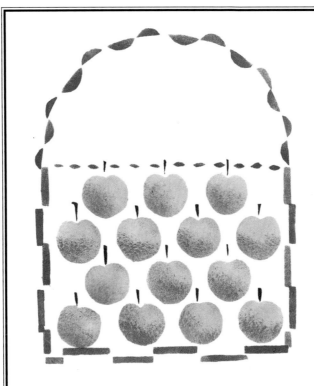

What we deem goodly order we're willing to state,
Eat hearty and decent, and clean out our plate;
Be thankful to heaven for what we receive,
And not make a mixture or compound to leave

We find of those bounties which heaven does give,
That some live to eat, and that some eat to live;
That some think of nothing but pleasing the taste,
And care very little how much they do waste.

FROM A TABLE 'MONITOR' POSTED IN THE DINING ROOM

CHAPTER ONE

SOUPS

Huge pots of stock, made from bones, trimmings and the cooking water from vegetables, simmered all day long and were used for nourishing soups – creamy chowders, smooth vegetable soups, broths with rice, and clear soups with vegetables and herbs. In the early days, soup often formed the main part of the meal at supper, with bread and butter, cheese and stewed fruit.

SPRING VEGETABLE AND HERB SOUP

The first young vegetables and herbs of spring were eagerly awaited after a long winter of cellared root vegetables, salted meats, dried fruits and other preserves.

4–6 SERVINGS

170 g/6 oz baby carrots (about 2 dozen), scrubbed or
peeled
170 g/6 oz baby leeks or spring onions (about 8) or
use button onions
15 g/½ oz butter
2 medium-size celery stalks, sliced
1.2 litres/2 pints good vegetable or chicken stock,
preferably home-made
140 g/5 oz baby courgettes (about 4), sliced
a large strip of lemon zest
2 teaspoons fresh thyme leaves
170 g/6 oz shelled fresh or frozen peas
4 large leaves of round lettuce, shredded
a handful of sorrel or baby spinach leaves, shredded
salt and pepper

Leave the carrots whole. Cut leeks or spring onions into pieces the same length as the carrots.

Melt the butter in a heavy saucepan and add the carrots, onions and celery. Cover and cook over a low heat for 5 minutes, stirring occasionally.

Pour in the stock and bring to the boil. Add the courgettes, lemon zest and thyme. Reduce the heat and leave to simmer for 20–30 minutes or until the vegetables are just tender.

Meanwhile, blanch fresh peas in boiling salted water for 2 minutes. Drain and refresh under cold running water. If using frozen peas, put them in a strainer and pour boiling water over them to thaw. Drain well.

Add the peas, lettuce and sorrel or spinach to the soup. Season with salt and pepper. Simmer for a further 1 minute. Discard the lemon zest and serve hot.

FRESH SWEETCORN CHOWDER

Manuscript recipes for fresh sweetcorn chowder were much richer than the modern version here: they used all cream and much more butter.

4 SERVINGS

4–6 ears of sweetcorn (to give 450 g/1 lb kernels)
30 g/1 oz butter
2 tablespoons flour
900 ml/1½ pints milk, or half milk and half chicken
stock
1–2 whole cloves
1 small onion, peeled
125 ml/4 fl oz whipping cream
a pinch of caster sugar
salt and pepper

Remove the green leaves and silk from the sweetcorn. With a sharp knife, cut the kernels from the cobs. Hold each cob upright in a shallow dish and scrape lengthways with the back of the knife to remove all the sweetcorn 'milk'. Set the kernels and sweetcorn milk aside.

Melt the butter in a heavy saucepan and stir in the flour. Cook, stirring, for 2–3 minutes. Gradually stir in the milk or milk and stock. Bring to the boil, stirring. Stick the cloves into the onion and add to the pan. Simmer for 5 minutes.

Add the sweetcorn kernels and milk, cream and sugar and season to taste. Bring back to the boil. Reduce the heat to low and simmer gently for about 30 minutes or until the sweetcorn is tender.

Discard the clove-studded onion. Taste the chowder for seasoning and serve very hot.

COOK'S NOTE If you prefer the sweetcorn to be softer in texture, blanch the kernels in boiling salted water for 2-3 minutes first.

SPICY BAKED BEAN SOUP

Nourishing and sustaining baked beans were a staple food in Shaker communities, just as they were in households in the World. Thus there were always leftover beans, and the inventive Shaker Sisters devised soups and other dishes to use them up.

4–6 SERVINGS

1 tablespoon vegetable oil
1 small onion, chopped
1–2 celery stalks, chopped
800 g/1¾ lb home-made slow-baked beans (page 85)
1 litre/1⅔ pints water
1 can (400 g/14 oz) chopped tomatoes with juice
¼ teaspoon dried hot red pepper flakes
salt and pepper

Heat the oil in a heavy saucepan, add the onion and celery and cook, stirring, until soft. Add the baked beans, water and tomatoes and stir well to mix. Add the pepper flakes. Bring to the boil, then cover and leave to simmer for 30 minutes.

Ladle the soup into a food processor and work until quite smooth, then rub it through a sieve into a clean saucepan. Alternatively use a food mill. Season with salt and pepper. Reheat the soup and serve hot.

POTATO AND LEEK SOUP

The 'pot liquor', or cooking water from vegetables, was never wasted, but was saved for soups, gravies and sauces, as well as for cooking noodles and dumplings. Here the caraway-infused potato pot liquor provides the base for a thick, hearty soup, which has a really good potato flavour. The recipe is based on one in *Mary Whitcher's Shaker House-Keeper*.

8 SERVINGS

1.35 kg/3 lb potatoes, all about the same size
1½ tablespoons caraway seeds
1 bay leaf
salt and pepper
450 g/1 lb leeks, trimmed and finely chopped
500 ml/16 fl oz single cream, or half milk and half cream
1 tablespoon chopped fresh thyme

Scrub the potatoes but don't peel them. Put them in a large saucepan with the caraway seeds, bay leaf and a large pinch of salt. Cover with plenty of cold water. Bring to the boil, then reduce the heat and simmer for about 20 minutes or until the potatoes are just tender when pierced with the tip of a knife.

Drain the potatoes in a colander set in a bowl and set them aside to cool. Strain the cooking liquid and reserve 1.5 litres/2⅓ pints.

When the potatoes are cool enough to handle, peel them and chop coarsely. Put them back in the saucepan with the reserved strained liquid. Add the leeks. Bring to the boil and simmer gently for about 30 minutes or until the leeks are soft.

Ladle the soup into a food processor and work until quite smooth but still with some texture. Return to the pan and stir in the cream and thyme. Season with salt and pepper. Reheat without boiling. Serve hot.

OVERLEAF: FRESH SWEETCORN CHOWDER (LEFT), CREAM OF SQUASH SOUP

CREAM OF SQUASH SOUP

The Native Americans introduced the first European settlers to pumpkin and other winter squashes. These useful vegetables could be harvested in the autumn and kept through the winter, thus being available to make warming soups and pie fillings. In early Shaker manuscripts pumpkin was called 'pompoon', which probably came from 'pompion' or 'pumpion', a word used by the English in the seventeenth century.

6 SERVINGS

a 1.35 kg/3 lb piece of pumpkin or butternut squash
30 g/1 oz butter
1 Spanish onion, finely chopped
1.2 litres/2 pints good chicken stock, preferably home-made
1 teaspoon grated orange zest
2 teaspoons finely chopped fresh ginger or
½ teaspoon ground ginger
salt and pepper

Preheat the oven to 200°C/400°F/Gas 6.

Scoop the seeds and fibres out of the piece of pumpkin (if using butternut squash, cut it lengthways in half first). Put the squash, cut side down, on a lightly oiled baking tray. Bake for 50–60 minutes or until soft and collapsed. Leave the squash to cool slightly, then remove and discard the skin, scraping off all the flesh on to the baking tray. Set aside.

Melt the butter in a heavy saucepan. Add the onion, cover and cook over a very low heat until soft but not coloured, stirring occasionally. Add the pumpkin flesh with any juices on the baking tray and mash it coarsely with a fork or spoon. Pour in the stock and add the orange zest and ginger. Season with salt and pepper. Bring to the boil, then cover, reduce the heat and leave to simmer for 25–30 minutes.

Pour the soup into a food processor and work until smooth, then press through a fine sieve back into the saucepan. (If using butternut squash, you will not need to sieve the soup after processing it.) Alternatively, use a food mill. Reheat the soup briefly and check the seasoning before serving.

BEEF AND VEGETABLE SOUP

Frugal home-makers of the last century never discarded meat bones and trimmings, and the Shaker Sisters were no exception to this golden rule of good housekeeping. Bones were used to make bouillons and stocks to form the base for hearty soups.

8–10 SERVINGS

1.35 kg/3 lb meaty beef soup bones or use sliced beef shin or neck
1 veal knuckle (optional)
2.5 litres/4 pints water
2 large onions, chopped
2 large celery stalks, chopped, plus leaves if available
a handful of parsley sprigs
a small handful of fresh thyme sprigs
1 bay leaf
12 black peppercorns, slightly crushed with the side of a knife
2 whole cloves
3 carrots, diced
1 medium-size turnip, diced
2–3 boiling potatoes, diced
100 g/3½ oz cabbage, shredded
1 can (425 g/15 oz) butter beans, drained
salt and pepper

Put the bones in a large pot or saucepan and pour in the water. Bring to the boil, skimming off the foam that rises to the surface. When the foam has stopped rising, add half of the onion and celery. Reserve a few sprigs of parsley and thyme and add the remainder to the pot with the bay leaf, peppercorns and cloves. Reduce the heat, cover and leave to simmer for 3–3½ hours.

Remove the bones from the pot and set aside. Strain the bouillon through a colander set in a large bowl, then pour it through a fine sieve back into the pot.

Add the remaining onion and celery to the bouillon together with the diced vegetables. Bring to the boil, then simmer gently for about 30 minutes.

Meanwhile, take the meat from the bones and cut it into small chunks. Chop the reserved herbs.

Add the meat, chopped herbs, cabbage and butter beans to the soup. Season with salt and pepper. Simmer for a further 5 minutes or until all the vegetables are tender. Serve hot, with herb bread or rolls.

COOK'S NOTE If you can, let the strained bouillon cool, then lift off the layer of fat that will set on the surface.

OLD-FASHIONED CHICKEN SOUP WITH NOODLES

The chickens raised by Shaker communities in the last century would have had much more flavour than the birds we buy today, as their varied diet included the greens and bugs they foraged for themselves. The flocks were large, and mature laying hens and old roosters would have ended up in the soup pot. If you can find a boiling fowl, by all means use it for this soup. Otherwise, choose a free-range chicken.

6–8 SERVINGS

a 1.35–1.6 kg/3–3½ lb chicken, ideally a boiling fowl,
cut into pieces
3 large leeks, total weight about 700 g/1½ lb
a large sprig of fresh rosemary
a few sprigs of fresh parsley
1 bay leaf
2.5 litres/4 pints water
1 celery stalk, cut into 2 cm/¾ inch pieces
2–3 carrots, cut into 1.25 cm/½ inch slices
2 parsnips, cut into 1.25 cm/½ inch slices
salt and pepper
a large handful of fresh home-made noodles
(page 88)

Put the chicken pieces in a large saucepan. Cut the green tops off the leeks and chop coarsely. Set the white parts aside. Add the green tops to the pan with the herbs and pour in the water. Bring to the boil, skimming off the foam that rises to the surface. Reduce the heat to low, cover and leave to simmer for 1–1½ hours or until the chicken is very tender (a boiling fowl will take longer to cook).

Lift out the chicken pieces and set them aside. Strain the stock through a colander set in a bowl, then pour it through a fine sieve back into the pan. Skim off the fat from the surface of the stock. (If you have time, leave the stock to cool and then refrigerate it; the fat will set on the surface and can be lifted off.)

Cut the white parts of the leeks into 1.25 cm/½ inch slices and add to the stock with the celery, carrots and parsnips. Season with salt and pepper. Bring to the boil, then partially cover the pan and simmer for 20 minutes.

Meanwhile, remove the chicken meat from the bones, discarding all the skin and fat. Coarsely shred as much of the meat as you want for the soup; keep the remainder for sandwiches or salads.

Add the noodles to the soup. Bring back to the boil and cook for about 5 minutes or until just tender.

Add the shredded chicken meat to the soup just before the end of the noodles' cooking time. Check the seasoning before serving.

COOK'S NOTE If you prefer, use 85 g/3 oz dried wide egg noodles, and cook for the time given on the packet.

FISH CHOWDER

When first made in New England, chowders were very thick fish dishes, but by the nineteenth century they had become thick, chunky soups. Many Shaker recipes used cracker meal for thickening chowders.

6 SERVINGS

1.8 kg/4 lb white fish such as cod, haddock or hake,
filleted, bones and trimmings reserved
3 large onions, halved and sliced
2 whole cloves
a slice of lemon
1.2 litres/2 pints water
115 g/4 oz smoked streaky bacon, rind removed,
diced
30 g/1 oz butter
700 g/1½ lb boiling potatoes, diced
500 ml/16 fl oz milk
salt and pepper
soda crackers or water biscuits to serve

PREVIOUS PAGES: OLD-FASHIONED CHICKEN SOUP WITH NOODLES

> *The heads, backbones and tails of fish
> should be cooked with a dash of
> marjoram and thyme for half an hour
> and the liquid used in making
> sauces for fish or to use in chowders.*
>
> MARY WHITCHER'S SHAKER HOUSE-KEEPER

Skin the fish fillets and cut into 2 cm/³/₄ inch chunks; set aside. Put the fish bones and trimmings in a heavy saucepan and add one of the sliced onions, the cloves and lemon slice. Pour in the water. Bring to the boil, then reduce the heat and leave to simmer gently for 20 minutes.

Strain the fish stock through a colander set in a large bowl, then pour it through a fine sieve. Reserve 1 litre/1²/₃ pints of the stock.

Put the bacon in a large saucepan with a knob of the butter and cook over a low heat until the bacon is browned. Lift out the bacon with a slotted spoon and drain on paper towels. Pour most of the fat from the pan, leaving just a film.

Add the remaining onions to the pan and cook, stirring, until they are soft. Add the potatoes and stir to mix with the onions. Cook for 3–4 minutes, stirring occasionally. Pour in the fish stock and bring to the boil. Reduce the heat to low, cover and simmer for about 15 minutes or until the potatoes are just tender.

Stir in the milk and bring back to the boil. Add the fish. Cook gently, uncovered, for about 5 minutes or until the fish is opaque.

Return the browned bacon to the pan. Add the remaining butter and season with salt and pepper. Heat through gently without boiling. Serve hot.

COOK'S NOTE If you prefer a thicker chowder, before adding the fish use a spoon or fork to mash some of the potato against the side of the pan.

OYSTER STEW

Many ingredients that are expensive today were commonplace and cheap in the eighteenth and nineteenth centuries, oysters being a good example. When they were in season, in autumn and winter, oysters appeared often on Shaker tables, fried or used in soups, stews and pies, and were thought to be very nutritious. The recipe here is based on one from *Mary Whitcher's Shaker House-Keepe*r.

6 SERVINGS

*36 fresh oysters
85 g/3 oz butter
a large pinch of cayenne pepper
600 ml/1 pint milk, warmed
300 ml/¹/₂ pint whipping cream, warmed
salt and white pepper*

Open the oysters and tip them into a saucepan with all their liquor. Add the butter and cayenne. Cook over a low heat for 3–4 minutes or until the oysters are just firm and the edges are starting to curl.

Add the milk and cream and stir to mix. Season with salt and pepper. Cook for a further 1–2 minutes. Serve immediately.

COOK'S NOTE Sprinkle with chopped fresh chives or parsley if liked.

CHAPTER TWO

FISH, POULTRY AND MEAT

Meat was originally eaten at breakfast, later at midday dinner. The western communities raised herds of cattle, while eastern ones had dairy cattle and flocks of sheep. All communities had pigs and chickens, kept in clean, well-ventilated conditions, and fresh fish was caught in ponds and lakes. Before refrigeration, fresh meat had to be eaten as quickly as possible, or it was salted, smoked or used to make sausage or brawn.

FISH AND EGGS

In *The Best of Shaker Cooking*, Amy Bess Miller and Persis Fuller note that this dish of fish, eggs and rich milk or cream was a favourite in all Shaker communities. Mary Whitcher gives a recipe using salt cod and cream, and garnishes it with chopped hard-boiled egg. The recipe here combines smoked and fresh fish, for a particularly delicious flavour.

4–6 SERVINGS

225 g/8 oz fresh cod fillet
225 g/8 oz smoked haddock fillet or use other smoked fish
500 ml/16 fl oz rich whole milk or half milk and half cream
a slice of onion
1 bay leaf
a few black peppercorns
15–30 g/½–1 oz butter
salt and pepper
900 g/2 lb potatoes, cooked and thinly sliced
4 hard-boiled eggs, sliced

Preheat the oven to 180°C/350°F/Gas 4.

Put the cod and smoked haddock in a shallow baking dish and add the milk or milk and cream mixture, onion slice, bay leaf and peppercorns. Cover the dish with a lid or foil and put it in the oven. Poach the fish for 15–20 minutes or until it is just firm and will almost flake.

Remove the fish to a plate. Strain the poaching milk through a fine sieve set in a bowl. Add the butter and season with salt and pepper. When the fish is cool enough to handle, break it into large flakes, discarding any skin and bones.

Wipe out the baking dish and butter it. Make a layer of potato slices on the bottom. Scatter over a layer of fish and cover with a layer of egg slices. Repeat the layers until the ingredients are used up, finishing with a layer of potatoes. Pour the warm milk mixture over the top.

Bake in the preheated oven for about 40 minutes or until piping hot and the milk has been absorbed. Serve in the baking dish.

CODFISH BALLS

The seaports of New England, particularly in Massachusetts, grew rich on the cod trade, and dried codfish were shipped by the hundreds of thousands to Europe as early as 1623. In common with other cooks in the late eighteenth and early nineteenth centuries, Shaker Sisters used this dried fish in chowders, stews, pies and traditional codfish balls. In some Shaker recipes the fish is not soaked, which suggests either that it was not as heavily salted as that sold today or that a very salty taste was preferred.

4–6 SERVINGS

340 g/12 oz salt cod fillets
450 g/1 lb potatoes, peeled and diced
1 egg, beaten
a large pinch of grated nutmeg
pepper
oil for frying
lemon wedges for serving

Put the salt cod fillets in a bowl of cold water and leave to soak for 12–24 hours. Change the soaking water several times. When ready, the fish should feel soft, similar to fresh cod. Drain well and flake the fish, discarding any skin.

Put the flaked fish and potatoes in a saucepan and cover with fresh cold water. Bring to the boil, then reduce the heat and simmer for 12–15 minutes or until the potatoes are tender.

Drain the fish and potatoes and return them to the pan. Cover with a crumpled tea towel and set aside for a few minutes: the towel will absorb the moisture in the steam, leaving the potatoes dry.

Beat the potatoes and fish together until quite smooth. Beat in the egg, nutmeg and pepper to taste.

Heat 5–7.5 cm/2–3 inches of oil in a large frying pan until it is very hot (190°C/375°F on a deep frying thermometer). Drop the fish mixture into the hot oil in spoonfuls to make balls about the size of a small egg. Fry until the balls are puffy and golden brown, turning to colour them evenly.

Drain the fish balls on paper towels and serve hot, with lemon wedges or crisply fried bacon.

BOILED FISH WITH A RICH SAUCE

The fish here is not actually boiled but is gently poached in a flavoured liquid. In some Shaker recipes, the liquid was thickened by whisking it into 3 or more whole eggs or egg yolks, which requires skill as this sort of mixture can easily curdle.

4 SERVINGS

250 ml/8 fl oz dry cider or white wine
750 ml/1¼ pints water
1 onion, finely chopped
1 celery stalk, finely chopped
2 carrots, finely chopped
1 bay leaf
a few fresh thyme sprigs
4 fish steaks, cut 2 cm/¾ inch thick
2 teaspoons cornflour mixed with 1 tablespoon cold water
1 egg yolk, lightly beaten with 2 tablespoons whipping cream
salt and pepper
3–4 tablespoons chopped fresh chives

Combine the cider or wine and water in a frying pan or other shallow pan large enough to accommodate the fish steaks. Add the chopped vegetables, bay leaf and thyme

sprigs. Bring to the boil, then reduce the heat and simmer gently for 20 minutes.

Put the fish into the liquid. Simmer very gently for about 8 minutes or until the fish is cooked. To test make a slit with a sharp knife: the flesh next to the bone should still be slightly translucent.

Lift the fish out of the liquid on to a platter and keep warm. Boil the cooking liquid until it has reduced to about 175 ml/6 fl oz. Strain it into a saucepan. Bring back to the boil, then whisk in the cornflour mixture. Whisk until thickened. Whisk a spoonful of the thickened sauce into the egg yolk mixture, then add this to the remaining sauce in the pan. Bring just to the boil, whisking. Season with salt and pepper and stir in the chives.

Spoon the sauce over the fish steaks and serve.

COOK'S NOTE You could prepare a whole fish or piece of a large fish in the same way, allowing 25–30 minutes cooking (according to thickness).

OVERLEAF: FISH AND EGGS (LEFT), CODFISH BALLS

BAKED FISH WITH HERB STUFFING

Some Shaker recipes for baked fish used fish stock to bind the cracker meal stuffing, and covered the fish with salt pork for baking.

6–8 SERVINGS

a whole fish weighing 1.8–2.25 kg/4–5 lb, cleaned and scaled if necessary
100 g/3½ oz water biscuits or cream crackers, crushed
2–3 tablespoons finely chopped fresh parsley
a small handful of fresh dill, chopped
1 small garlic clove, finely chopped (optional)
45 g/1½ oz butter, melted
salt and pepper
1 egg, beaten
cornmeal
4–6 streaky bacon rashers

Preheat the oven to 180°C/350°F/Gas 4.

Remove the head and tail from the fish. It can then be boned or cut into two fillets. Keep all the trimmings for making a fish stock, if liked. Rinse the fish under cold running water and pat dry with paper towels.

Mix together the cracker crumbs, herbs, garlic and butter. Season with salt and pepper. Bind with the egg.

Stuff the boned fish with the herb mixture; or spread the mixture over one fish fillet and set the other fillet on top, to reshape the fish. 'Sew' the opening(s) closed with metal skewers or wooden cocktail sticks. Lay the fish in a buttered baking dish and dredge lightly with cornmeal. Score three or four diagonal slashes on the top side. Lay the bacon rashers evenly over the fish. Pour a little water, fish stock or white wine into the dish.

Bake for 35–40 minutes, basting occasionally with the liquid in the dish. To test if the fish is cooked, make a slit into the flesh with a sharp knife: the flesh should still be slightly translucent in the centre. Serve hot.

FRIED CHICKEN WITH CREAM GRAVY

The method of coating chicken pieces with seasoned flour or batter and then frying them in hot fat until crisp and golden brown originated in the South, possibly introduced by the Scots who settled there. It gradually made its way northwards, where the Shaker Sisters no doubt tried it and found it delicious, particularly when paired with a gravy made from the rich cream produced in the Shaker dairies.

6 SERVINGS

2 chickens, each weighing about 1.1 kg/2½ lb, cut into pieces
85 g/3 oz plain flour
½ teaspoon salt
½ teaspoon pepper
½ teaspoon paprika
½ teaspoon dried marjoram or oregano
30 g/1 oz butter
3 tablespoons bacon fat, lard or vegetable oil
250 ml/8 fl oz cream, or half milk and half cream

Rinse the chicken pieces and pat dry with paper towels. Put the flour, salt, pepper, paprika and marjoram in a plastic bag and shake to mix. Add the chicken pieces, two or three at a time, and shake to coat with the seasoned flour. Shake off excess flour and set the pieces on a rack.

Heat the butter and fat or oil in a large heavy frying pan over moderately high heat. When the fat is hot, put in the chicken pieces, in one layer (fry in batches if necessary). Fry until well browned, turning so the pieces colour evenly.

Remove the chicken pieces and reserve. Pour excess fat from the pan. Add the cream or cream and milk mixture to the pan and stir to mix with the sediments. Return the chicken pieces. Cover and cook over a low heat for 20–25 minutes or until the chicken is cooked and tender.

Transfer the chicken to a platter. Whisk the cream gravy to blend it evenly, and check the seasoning. Pour the gravy over the chicken and serve.

CHESTNUT AND HERB STUFFING FOR TURKEY

At one time, chestnut trees grew in great forests all the way from Maine to Alabama, and chestnuts were used by Shaker cooks in both sweet and savoury dishes. Unfortunately, nearly all the native trees were killed by a chestnut blight in 1904, and it took over 30 years for them to recover.

MAKES ENOUGH TO STUFF A 4.5–5.4 KG/10–12 LB TURKEY

225 g/8 oz butter
3 large onions, finely chopped
3 large celery stalks with leaves, finely chopped
about 250 ml/8 fl oz boiling water
340 g/12 oz day-old bread, crumbled or cubed
2 tablespoons chopped fresh thyme
2 tablespoons chopped fresh marjoram
1 tablespoon chopped fresh rosemary
255 g/9 oz freshly cooked or canned chestnuts,
chopped
salt and pepper
2 eggs, beaten

Melt 55 g/2 oz of the butter in a heavy frying pan. Add the onions and celery and cook over moderate heat until the vegetables are soft but not brown. Remove from the heat and leave to cool slightly.

Put the remaining butter in a bowl, pour in the boiling water and stir to melt the butter. Add the bread and toss with a fork to moisten.

Add the softened vegetables to the bowl together with the herbs and chestnuts. Season with salt and pepper. Add the eggs and mix well. Leave to cool before stuffing the turkey.

COOK'S NOTE The stuffing can also be baked in a buttered dish, covered, in 180–190°C/350–375°F/Gas 4–5 oven for 30–45 minutes.

CHICKEN BREASTS WITH FRIED APPLES

Visitors from the World, who came to enjoy a meal at the bountiful Shaker table, would often be served chicken, and they always remembered how yellow and rich the meat was.

4 SERVINGS

30 g/1 oz butter
2 tart green apples such as Granny Smith's, cored
and sliced across into rings
1 tablespoon vegetable oil
4 skinless boneless chicken breasts
4 tablespoons dry apple cider
1 teaspoon grated lemon zest
4 tablespoons whipping cream
salt and pepper

Heat the butter in a heavy frying pan over moderately low heat. Add the apple rings and turn to coat with butter. Fry for about 15 minutes or until tender and very lightly browned, turning occasionally. Remove the apples with a fish slice and drain on paper towels. Keep warm.

Add the oil to the pan and heat over moderately high heat. When hot, add the chicken breasts and cook for 2–3 minutes on each side or until golden brown.

Add the cider and lemon zest and bring to the boil. Cover and simmer over moderate heat for 5–10 minutes or until the chicken is cooked and tender.

Remove the chicken from the pan and keep warm. Add the cream and bring the liquid back to the boil. Season with salt and pepper. Boil for 1–2 minutes or until reduced to a saucelike consistency.

Pour the sauce over the chicken, garnish with the fried apple rings and serve.

CHICKEN POTPIE

The Shakers raised large flocks of chickens, and no part of the bird was ever wasted. The fat was rendered to use as a substitute for butter in chicken dishes as well as in pastries, cookies, puddings and scone-like 'biscuits'.

6 SERVINGS

45 g/1½ oz butter
1 onion, finely chopped
1 celery stalk, thinly sliced
225 g/8 oz mushrooms, quartered
3 tablespoons flour
500 ml/16 fl oz rich chicken stock, preferably home-made
125 ml/4 fl oz single cream
1 tablespoon chopped fresh parsley
255 g/9 oz shelled fresh or thawed frozen peas
400 g/14 oz cooked chicken, diced
salt and pepper

FOR THE TOP

255 g/9 oz plain flour
85 g/3 oz strong plain flour
1 tablespoon baking powder
½ teaspoon salt
½ teaspoon caster sugar
85 g/3 oz cold butter
1 tablespoon finely chopped fresh rosemary
about 175 ml/6 fl oz buttermilk

Preheat the oven to 220°C/425°F/Gas 7.

Melt 15 g/½ oz of the butter in a saucepan, add the onion, celery and mushrooms and cook over a low heat until softened. With a slotted spoon, remove the vegetables from the pan and set aside. Melt the remaining butter in the pan, stir the flour and cook, stirring, for about 2 minutes. Gradually stir in the stock and bring to the boil. Simmer gently for 5–10 minutes.

Meanwhile, make the dough for the top. Sift the flours, baking powder, salt and sugar into a bowl. Rub in the butter until coarse crumbs are formed. Add the rosemary. Gradually mix in the buttermilk to make a soft dough, kneading as little as possible. Roll out the dough to about 1.25 cm/½ inch thickness.

Stir the cream and parsley into the sauce. Add the peas, chicken and softened vegetables. Season with salt and pepper. Pour the mixture into a 1.5 litre/2⅓ pint baking dish or casserole that is at least 5 cm/2 inches deep. Lay the rolled-out dough over the top and press on to the rim of the dish. Crimp or fork the edge if liked. Cut three or four slashes in the top.

Bake for 25–30 minutes or until the top is risen and golden brown and the filling is bubbling. Serve hot.

COOK'S NOTE The dough can also be cut into 5 cm/2 inch rounds, placed on a buttered baking sheet and baked at 230°C/450°F/Gas 8 for 10–12 minutes, to make baking powder 'biscuits'.

PREVIOUS PAGES: CHICKEN POTPIE (LEFT), CHICKEN BREASTS WITH FRIED APPLES

HOT TURKEY OR CHICKEN AND MUSHROOM SANDWICHES

Although primarily observed as a religious day of forgiving, Christmas was joyfully celebrated in Shaker communities, and the dining room was festooned with wreaths and garlands. A feast was enjoyed at Thanksgiving too, with roast chicken normally given pride of place. Recipes for using up the leftovers were always being devised by the Shaker Sisters.

6 SERVINGS

55 g/2 oz turkey or chicken dripping or butter
1 large onion, finely chopped
450 g/1 lb mushrooms, trimmed and sliced
3½ tablespoons flour
500 ml/16 fl oz turkey or chicken stock made from the carcass
2 teaspoons finely chopped fresh thyme
a large dash of Worcestershire sauce or more to taste
salt and pepper
340 g/12 oz cooked turkey or chicken, cut into medium-thick slices
6 thick slices of bread, buttered if liked

Heat the dripping or butter in a wide pan, add the onion and mushrooms and cook over moderate heat until the onion is soft and the mushrooms are wilted (they will exude liquid). Sprinkle over the flour and stir in well, then gradually stir in the stock. Bring to the boil, stirring. Add the thyme and Worcestershire sauce, and season with salt and pepper. Leave to simmer gently for 10 minutes, stirring frequently.

Put the slices of turkey or chicken into the mushroom gravy (add them one at a time so they are coated on both sides) and heat through for 2–3 minutes.

Divide the sliced turkey or chicken among the bread slices. Spoon the mushroom gravy over the top and serve immediately.

MEAT LOAF

As cooks were advised on a Shaker sales leaflet, herbs 'give character to food and add charm and variety to ordinary dishes'. That is certainly the case with an ordinary dish such as meat loaf.

4–6 SERVINGS

450 g/1 lb lean minced beef
225 g/8 oz minced veal
225 g/8 oz minced pork
1 small onion, finely chopped
2 tablespoons finely chopped fresh parsley
2 teaspoons chopped fresh thyme
2 teaspoons chopped fresh sage
1 teaspoon salt or more to taste
¼ teaspoon pepper or more to taste
1 egg
175 ml/6 fl oz half cream or milk
1½ teaspoons prepared mustard
25 g/scant 1 oz water biscuit crumbs or breadcrumbs
5 tablespoons beef stock

Preheat the oven to 180°C/350°F/Gas 4.

Combine the meats, onion, herbs, salt and pepper in a bowl. In another bowl, lightly beat the egg with the half cream or milk and mustard. Add the crumbs and stir to mix. Add the crumb mixture to the meat mixture and toss together, using a fork to blend the ingredients lightly but thoroughly.

Spoon the meat mixture into the centre of a shallow baking tin and shape into a long bolster shape, pressing together firmly but gently. Pour the stock around the meat loaf. Bake for 1½ hours or until browned and cooked through, basting occasionally with the juices in the tin. Leave to rest for 5–10 minutes before cutting into slices.

COOK'S NOTE If you prefer, use 700 g/1½ lb beef with 225 g/8 oz pork or wild boar.

BEEF STEW WITH HERB DUMPLINGS

The Shakers could savour their home-raised grass-fed beef in stews such as this.

6 SERVINGS

flour
salt and pepper
900 g/2 lb braising or stewing steak, cut into
4 cm/1½ inch cubes
15 g/½ oz butter
2 tablespoons vegetable oil
1 litre/1⅔ pints hot water
8–12 small or button onions, peeled
4 carrots, cut into 1.25 cm/½ inch pieces
3 celery stalks, cut into 2.5 cm/1 inch pieces
2 turnips or parsnips, cut into 1.25 cm/½ inch pieces
450 g/1 lb small boiling potatoes, peeled

FOR THE DUMPLINGS

85 g/3 oz yellow cornmeal
85 g/3 oz plain flour
1 teaspoon baking powder
¾ teaspoon salt
3 tablespoons chopped mixed fresh herbs, eg parsley,
thyme, lovage, marjoram
1 egg, beaten
125 ml/4 fl oz milk
15 g/½ oz butter, melted

Season some flour with salt and pepper and use to coat the cubes of beef; shake off excess flour. Heat the butter with the oil in a wide flameproof casserole. When the fat is very hot, add the beef cubes and brown them on all sides. Do this in batches and keep the heat quite high. When all the beef cubes have been browned, pour in the water and bring to the boil. Reduce the heat, cover the casserole and simmer for about 2 hours or until the beef is almost tender.

Add the vegetables and stir to mix. Season with salt and pepper. Bring back to the boil, then cover again and leave to simmer over low heat for about 30 minutes.

Meanwhile, prepare the dumpling batter. Combine the cornmeal, flour, baking powder, salt and herbs in a bowl. Add the egg, milk and butter and stir to make a thick batter.

Drop the batter in 6 large spoonfuls on top of the stew. Cover and simmer for about 15 minutes or until the dumplings are puffed and firm to the touch and the meat and vegetables are tender. Serve hot.

COOK'S NOTE Cubes of boneless venison could be substituted for the beef.

POT ROAST WITH HORSERADISH SAUCE

Shaker cooks wasted nothing – even the toughest cuts of meat from work animals would have been used in a bouillon or soup, or slowly pot roasted until tender. Beef today doesn't need the same amount of slow cooking to make it appetizing, but pot roasting still gives succulent and delicious results.

6–8 SERVINGS

2 tablespoons beef dripping or vegetable oil
a 1.35 kg/3 lb boneless beef joint such as topside, any
fat removed

1 Spanish onion, chopped
4 tablespoons cider vinegar
2 tablespoons cranberry catsup (page 134)
250 ml/8 fl oz beef stock or water
3 whole cloves
salt and pepper

FOR THE SAUCE

125 ml/4 fl oz whipping cream
1 teaspoon dry mustard
1 teaspoon caster sugar
4 tablespoons freshly grated horseradish
2 tablespoons mayonnaise
salt and pepper

Heat the dripping or oil in a flameproof casserole into which the beef joint will just fit comfortably. When the fat is hot, put in the beef. Brown it well on all sides over a brisk heat, turning with two spoons. Lift out the joint and reserve.

Add the onion to the casserole and stir to mix with the fat. Cook over a moderately low heat until soft and beginning to brown. Stir in the vinegar, cranberry catsup and stock or water. Add the cloves and season with salt and pepper. Bring to the boil.

Put the beef joint back in the casserole. Cover and cook over a low heat for 2–2½ hours or until the beef is tender.

Meanwhile, make the sauce. Mix a little cream with the mustard and sugar until smooth. Add the remaining cream and whip until thick. Stir in the horseradish and mayonnaise and season with salt and pepper. Cover and refrigerate.

Transfer the beef to a carving board and keep warm. Simmer the cooking liquid, uncovered, until reduced to about 250 ml/8 fl oz. Strain and check the seasoning.

Slice the beef and serve with the gravy and horseradish sauce.

COOK'S NOTE If you prefer a thickened gravy, whisk in 1–2 teaspoons cornflour mixed with 1 tablespoon cold water.

OVERLEAF: POT ROAST WITH HORSERADISH SAUCE

PORK CHOPS IN SOURED CREAM

Making apple cider was a traditional autumn activity in Shaker communities, and the freshly pressed juice was kept in cool cellars to prevent it from fermenting into an alcoholic beverage too quickly.

4 SERVINGS

4 loin pork chops, weighing 200–225 g/7–8 oz each,
well trimmed
dry mustard
salt and pepper
a small knob of butter
½ tablespoon vegetable oil
1 carrot, diced
1 celery stalk, diced
1 small onion, chopped
250 ml/8 fl oz dry cider, or half chicken stock and half
cider
125 ml/4 fl oz thick soured cream

Season the chops on both sides with mustard, salt and pepper. Heat the butter and oil in a heavy frying pan just large enough to accommodate the chops. Add the chops and brown quickly on both sides. Scatter the vegetables over and around the chops, then cover the pan and reduce the heat to low. Cook for 10 minutes.

Turn the chops over. Add the cider to the pan and bring to the boil. Cover the pan again and simmer for 20–25 minutes or until the chops are cooked through and tender. Turn the chops once or twice.

Remove the chops from the pan to a warmed serving platter and keep hot. Boil the cooking liquid, uncovered, until reduced to about 4 tablespoons. Strain into a saucepan, pressing well on the vegetables. Reheat the strained liquid just to boiling, then whisk in the soured cream. Season with salt and pepper. Pour the sauce over

LAMB AND BARLEY STEW

The Shakers kept flocks of sheep both for meat and for wool. In the spring, young and tender lamb would be enjoyed; older animals provided mutton, and there are many recipes for mutton in Shaker manuscripts. This distinctively flavoured meat is not easily obtainable today, but if available it can be used in this hearty stew.

4 SERVINGS

15 g/½ oz butter
1 tablespoon vegetable oil
700 g/1½ lb boneless lamb shoulder, trimmed of excess fat and cut into cubes
2 onions, chopped
1–2 celery stalks, chopped
4–5 carrots, cut into chunks
100 g/3½ oz pearl barley
600 ml/1 pint chicken stock or water
1 bay leaf
1–2 teaspoons Worcestershire sauce
salt and pepper

Heat the butter and oil in a flameproof casserole. Add the cubes of lamb and brown them quickly on all sides; do this in batches if necessary. Remove the lamb with a slotted spoon and set aside.

Add the vegetables to the casserole, reduce the heat and fry, stirring, until the onion is soft and starting to brown. Add the barley and stir well to mix. Pour in the stock or water and add the bay leaf and Worcestershire sauce. Return the lamb cubes to the pot and season with salt and pepper. Bring to the boil, then cover and reduce the heat. Cook for about 1 hour or until the lamb and barley are tender.

LAMB STEAKS WITH HERB BUTTER

The Shaker Sisters used the herbs from their garden in so many ways, both culinary and medicinal. In the kitchen, they blended dried herbs to make seasoning mixes, and mixed fresh herbs into soft butter to be used as spreads for warm breads and rolls as well as in cooking.

4 SERVINGS

55 g/2 oz soft butter
2 teaspoons finely chopped fresh parsley
1 teaspoon finely chopped fresh thyme
1 teaspoon finely chopped fresh mint
1 teaspoon prepared mustard, preferably Dijon
a few drops of lemon juice
salt and pepper
4 lamb steaks cut from the leg

Combine the butter, herbs, mustard and lemon juice in a bowl and beat well together. Season with salt and pepper. Set aside.

Salt and pepper the lamb steaks, then cook them over charcoal, on a cast-iron ridged grill pan or under the grill. Top each steak with a spoonful of herb butter and serve immediately.

COOK'S NOTE You can also serve the herb butter on thick lamb chops or beef steaks (omitting the mint if preferred).

LAMB KNUCKLES WITH DRIED FRUIT

Sauces and gravies for Shaker dishes were rarely prepared European-style, but rather were based on the juices produced in the cooking.

4 SERVINGS

4 lamb knuckles
salt and pepper
2 small onions, quartered
400 ml/14 fl oz chicken stock or water
100 g/3½ oz plump tenderized prunes
55 g/2 oz plump tenderized dried apricot halves
40 g/1½ oz dried unsweetened cranberries
6 whole allspice
4 whole cloves
1 bay leaf

Preheat the oven to 180°C/350°F/Gas 4.

Arrange the lamb knuckles in a heavy baking dish or casserole, in one layer if possible. Season the knuckles with salt and pepper. Tuck in the onion quarters. Add 4 tablespoons of the stock or water. Cover tightly and put into the oven. Cook for 1 hour.

Combine the remaining ingredients, with the rest of the stock or water, in a saucepan and bring to the boil. Remove from the heat and set aside.

Add the fruit mixture to the baking dish. Cover and return to the oven. Cook for about 1 hour or until the lamb is very tender and falling from the bones and the fruit is very soft and plump. Skim the fat from the cooking liquid before serving.

HAM BAKED IN CIDER

In American cookery books in the late eighteenth and early nineteenth centuries there was much emphasis on pickling, and all rural home-makers produced their own brined or smoked meats. The Shakers excelled at preserving perishables, and were particulary known for their excellent smoked gammon hams.

10 OR MORE SERVINGS

½ fully cooked gammon ham, weighing
2.25–3 kg/5–7 lb
whole cloves
500 ml/16 fl oz dry cider
125 ml/4 fl oz water
2 tablespoons light soft brown sugar
a large strip of lemon zest

Preheat the oven to 170°C/325°F/Gas 3.

If there is any rind on the ham, remove it and trim off excess fat. Score the remaining surface fat in large diamond shapes, cutting through the fat and just into the flesh. Stick a clove in the centre of each diamond. Set the ham in a roasting tin.

Combine the remaining ingredients in a saucepan and bring to the boil, stirring. Simmer for 5 minutes.

Discard the lemon zest, then pour the mixture over the ham. Bake for about 1½ hours or until the ham is hot all the way through, basting frequently with the cider mixture in the tin. (The internal temperature of the ham should be 68°C/155°F on a meat thermometer.)

Transfer the ham to a carving board and keep warm. Pour the cider mixture into a saucepan. Skim off surface fat, then bring to the boil and boil until syrupy. Brush this syrupy glaze over the ham and leave for a few minutes before carving.

OVERLEAF: LAMB STEAKS WITH HERB BUTTER (LEFT), HAM AND POTATO HASH

BACON AND EGG HAND PIES

For the Shakers, picnics were much-anticipated treats, and small savoury pies usually formed part of the repast.

MAKES 4

4 smoked back bacon rashers, rind removed
vegetable oil
4 eggs, size 5 or 6
pepper
1 egg yolk beaten with 2 teaspoons water

FOR THE PASTRY

340 g/12 oz plain flour
½ teaspoon salt
1½ teaspoons dry mustard
115 g/4 oz cold butter, cut into pieces
55 g/2 oz mature Cheddar cheese or other firm well-flavoured cheese, grated
5–7 tablespoons cold water

First make the pastry. Put the flour, salt and mustard in the food processor and turn on the machine briefly to mix. Add the butter and process until the mixture resembles crumbs, turning the machine on and off several times. Add the cheese and process briefly. Add enough water to bind the ingredients (they should still look crumbly), then turn on to the work surface and mix briefly with your hands to a smooth dough. Gather into a ball, wrap and refrigerate for at least 30 minutes.

Fry the bacon in a film of vegetable oil until it is crisp and browned. Drain on paper towels, then chop coarsely.

Preheat the oven to 200°C/400°F/Gas 6.

Divide the dough into eight equal pieces. Using a saucer as a guide, roll out one piece of dough to a round that is a little larger than the saucer. Dust the saucer with flour, then line it with the round of dough. Scatter in a crumbled rasher of bacon and make a little well in the centre. Break an egg over the top, centring the yolk in

the well. Season with pepper. Roll out a second piece of dough to make the top crust. Press the edges together to seal, then roll them over together, pressing well. (Be sure to seal well or the egg will escape.) Make one or two small slits in the top crust. Transfer the pie to a baking sheet. Make three more pies in the same way.

Brush the tops of the pies with the egg yolk glaze. Bake for about 20 minutes or until golden brown and crisp. Serve hot or cold.

HAM AND POTATO HASH

4 SERVINGS

30 g/1 oz butter
1–2 tablespoons vegetable oil
1 Spanish onion, finely chopped
700 g/1½ lb boiling potatoes, peeled and diced
225 g/8 oz cooked ham, finely chopped
2 eggs, beaten
1–2 teaspoons prepared mustard
salt and pepper

Heat half of the butter with 1 tablespoon oil in a heavy non-stick frying pan. Add the onion and potatoes and cook until tender and lightly browned, stirring frequently.

Turn the onion and potatoes into a bowl and add the ham, eggs and mustard. Season with salt and pepper. Mix well.

Heat the remaining butter in the frying pan, with more oil if necessary. Spoon in the ham and potato mixture and spread out evenly, pressing down into a cake. Cook for about 5 minutes or until browned on the base. Then turn over and brown the other side (or brown under the grill without turning). Cut into wedges to serve.

COOK'S NOTE You could substitute left-over cooked potatoes, adding them to the onion with the ham.

CHAPTER THREE

VEGETARIAN DISHES

At a time when the World's people were eating meals that contained lots of meat, much of it salted, and drinking copious amounts of spirits, the Shakers adopted a vegetarian regime. It was not rigidly enforced in all the communities, but the kitchen Sisters devised such appetizing meatless fare that it would have been appealing to all but the most traditional of Believers.

LENTIL LOAF

4–6 SERVINGS

400 g/14 oz green lentils
30 g/1 oz finely chopped onion
1 garlic clove, finely chopped (optional)
1 tablespoon chopped fresh parsley
1 tablespoon chopped fresh sage
2 teaspoons chopped fresh thyme
salt and pepper
140 g/5 oz mature Cheddar cheese, grated
40 g/1½ oz fresh breadcrumbs
30 g/1 oz walnuts, chopped
1 egg, beaten
melted butter

FOR THE TOMATO SAUCE

900 g/2 lb ripe tomatoes, seeded and chopped
15 g/½ oz butter
½–1 teaspoon caster sugar
3–4 tablespoons grated fresh horseradish

Put the lentils in a saucepan, cover with cold water and bring to the boil. Reduce the heat and simmer until the lentils are very soft. Drain well and leave to cool.

Preheat the oven to 180°C/350°F/Gas 4.

Combine the lentils, onion, garlic and herbs in a bowl. Season with salt and pepper. Add 115 g/4 oz of the cheese, the crumbs and walnuts and mix well together. Mix in the egg to bind the ingredients.

Spoon the mixture on to the centre of a lightly greased baking tin and mould the mixture into a flattened loaf shape, pressing firmly. Brush the loaf all over with melted butter and scatter the remaining cheese over the top.

Bake for about 45 minutes or until firm and lightly browned.

Meanwhile, make the tomato sauce. Put the tomatoes and butter in a heavy saucepan and simmer for about 20 minutes or until very soft and reduced. Purée in a blender or food processor, then press through a fine sieve and return to the pan. Stir in the sugar and season with salt and pepper. Add the horseradish and set aside.

Leave the lentil loaf to cool for 5 minutes, then slice and serve with the warm tomato sauce.

Vegetarianism is not yet incorporated into the Society, although beyond all doubt it is destined someday to become so. But in our Family there are quite a number of vegetarians, and I enjoy the privilege, which I dearly prize, of eating at a table bounteously spread with good nourishing food, but unpolluted with the products of the shambles in any shape or form...

FROM *SHAKER AND SHAKERESS*, NOVEMBER, 1873

VEGETABLE POTPIE

The potpie – truly an American classic – usually has a chicken, beef or pork filling. But during the time of the Shakers' 'bloodless diet', only vegetables would have been used.

4–6 SERVINGS

30 g/1 oz butter
1 large onion, sliced
1 tart green apple, peeled, cored and chopped
2 tablespoons flour
300 ml/½ pint milk
salt and pepper
2 carrots, cut into 5 mm/¼ inch slices
2 celery stalks, cut into 5 mm/¼ inch slices
170 g/6 oz swede, cut into small cubes
3 medium-size boiling potatoes, cut into small cubes
cheese pastry for a double-crust pie (page 62, Bacon and Egg Hand Pies)

Melt the butter in a saucepan, add the onion and fry until soft but not browned. Stir in the apple and cook for 1 minute, then stir in the flour. Cook for a further 1–2 minutes, stirring constantly. Gradually stir in the milk and bring to the boil. Simmer very gently for about 5 minutes, stirring occasionally. Season with salt and pepper. Set aside.

Steam the carrots, celery, swede and potatoes until just tender. Add to the onion and apple sauce. Stir to mix. Leave to cool slightly.

Preheat the oven to 200°C/400°F/Gas 6.

On a lightly floured surface, roll out two-thirds of the pastry dough thinly and use to line a shallow 1.5 litre/2⅓ pint casserole. Fill with the vegetable mixture. Roll out the remaining pastry dough for the top crust and crimp the edges to seal. Cut a cross in the centre of the top crust to make a steam vent hole.

Bake for 40–45 minutes or until the pastry is golden brown. Serve hot.

ASPARAGUS AND CHEDDAR PUDDING

Savoury bread puddings were a very popular supper dish, being both economical and filling. The recipes were often just buttered bread, lots of cheese, eggs and cream – simple but delicious.

6 SERVINGS

340–450 g/¾–1 lb tender asparagus spears
8 slices of bread, crusts trimmed if liked
soft butter
115 g/4 oz mature Cheddar or other firm well-flavoured cheese, grated
1 teaspoon dry mustard
500 ml/16 fl oz milk or half milk and half cream
3 eggs
salt and pepper

Trim the tough ends from the asparagus spears, cutting the spears to fit the width of the baking dish (a 24 × 18 cm/ 9½ × 7½ inch dish works well). Lay the asparagus spears in a wide pan of boiling salted water. Bring the water back to the boil, then simmer for 6–8 minutes or until the asparagus is just tender. Lift out and drain on paper towels. Alternatively, steam the asparagus until tender.

Preheat the oven to 180°C/350°F/Gas 4.

Butter the slices of bread. Arrange half of them on the bottom of the baking dish, buttered side down. Trim the bread to fit if necessary. Lay the asparagus spears on top in one layer, alternating the direction the spears are pointing, and sprinkle with half of the cheese. Cover with the remaining bread slices, buttered side up, and sprinkle on the rest of the cheese.

Dissolve the mustard in 1 tablespoon milk in a bowl. Add the eggs and remaining milk and season with salt and pepper. Beat together lightly. Pour evenly over the bread in the baking dish, then press down so the top layer of bread is moistened.

Bake for 30–40 minutes or until puffy, golden brown and crisp on top. Serve hot.

TOMATO CREAM PIE

When tomatoes made their appearance in American cookery books, in the mid-nineteenth century, the instructions were to cook them for several hours to make sauces and catsups, but not to eat them raw. However, the Shakers were growing tomatoes as early as 1823, and enjoyed them raw, fried and baked in a delicious pie. They also bottled quantities of tomatoes for winter use.

6 SERVINGS

pastry for a double-crust pie (page 127, Lemon Pie, or your favourite recipe)
soft butter
700 g/1½ lb firm, well-flavoured tomatoes
1–1½ tablespoons light soft brown sugar or more to taste (according to the sweetness of the tomatoes)
¼ teaspoon grated nutmeg
about 1 teaspoon plain flour
salt and pepper
125 ml/4 fl oz whipping cream
1 egg

Preheat the oven to 190°C/375°F/Gas 5.

Roll out just over half of the pastry dough and use to line a 23 cm/9 inch pie plate that is about 5 cm/2 inches deep. Brush a film of soft butter over the bottom of the pastry case.

If the tomatoes have tough skins, you may want to peel them. Slice the tomatoes. Spread out the slices on paper towels and leave to drain for 5–10 minutes.

Layer the tomato slices in the pastry case, sprinkling each layer with brown sugar, nutmeg, flour, salt and pepper. Lightly beat the cream with the egg and pour over the tomatoes, filling the gaps between the slices.

Roll out the remaining pastry dough for the top crust and crimp the edges together to seal. Make a few small holes or slits in the top for steam vents. Bake the pie for 35–40 minutes or until the pastry is golden brown. Serve hot or at room temperature, from the pie plate.

SMOTHERED ONION PIE

Even after the experiment with vegetarianism came to an end, meatless dishes remained popular on Shaker tables.

6–8 SERVINGS

55 g/2 oz butter
2–3 large onions, total weight about 600 g/1¼ lb, thinly sliced
450 g/1 lb leeks, trimmed of dark green and thinly sliced
4 tablespoons finely chopped fresh parsley
salt and pepper
40 g/1½ oz fine breadcrumbs from day-old bread
75 g/2½ oz walnuts, chopped
2 eggs
175 ml/6 fl oz soured cream

FOR THE PASTRY

200 g/7 oz plain flour
¼ teaspoon salt
100 g/3½ oz cold butter, cut into pieces
3–4 tablespoons cold water
soft butter

Melt half of the butter in a heavy frying pan. Add the onions and leeks and cover the pan. Cook over moderately low heat for about 30 minutes or until the onions and leeks are very soft and light golden in colour. Stir from time to time.

While the onions and leeks are cooking, make the pastry. Put the flour and salt in the food processor and turn the machine on briefly to blend. Add the butter and process until the mixture resembles coarse crumbs, turning the machine on and off several times. Add enough water to bind the ingredients (the mixture should still look crumbly). Turn on to the work surface and mix briefly with your hands to make a smooth dough. Gather into a ball, wrap and refrigerate for 20 minutes.

Uncover the frying pan and cook briskly to evaporate

excess liquid from the onions and leeks, stirring. Remove from the heat and stir in the parsley. Season with salt and pepper. Set aside.

Preheat the oven to 190°C/375°F/Gas 5.

Roll out the pastry dough and use to line a 23 cm/9 inch pie plate that is about 5 cm/2 inches deep. Brush a film of soft butter over the bottom of the pastry case.

Melt the remaining butter in a small pan. Remove from the heat and stir in the crumbs. Add the walnuts. Set aside.

Spread the onion mixture in the pastry case. Lightly beat the eggs with the soured cream and pour over the onions. Scatter the buttered crumbs and walnuts on top.

Bake for 25–30 minutes or until the pastry is golden brown and the filling is just set. Serve hot or at room temperature, from the pie plate.

OVERLEAF: BAKED STUFFED ACORN SQUASH (LEFT), LENTIL LOAF

Fluffy Cheese and Chive Omelette

In the dairies the Shaker Sisters made cheeses of all kinds from cream and milk, both whole and skimmed. Many were flavoured with herbs.

4 SERVINGS

225 g/8 oz creamy soft cheese
4 tablespoons (10 g/⅓ oz) chopped fresh chives, with the chive flowers if available
salt and pepper
6 eggs, separated
a pinch of cream of tartar
1 tablespoon milk or water
30 g/1 oz butter

Preheat the oven to 180°C/350°F/Gas 4.

Mix the cheese with the chopped chives in a bowl. Season with salt and pepper. Set the bowl in a pan of hot water and leave to warm slightly, stirring occasionally.

In a large bowl, beat the egg whites until frothy. Add the cream of tartar and continue beating until the whites will hold stiff peaks. Put the egg yolks in another bowl and beat with the milk or water and some seasoning until pale and thickened. Add a large spoonful of the whites to the egg yolks and beat in lightly, then fold in the remaining whites gently but thoroughly.

Melt the butter in a large frying pan (26–30 cm/10½–12 inches in diameter) with an ovenproof handle. Pour in the egg mixture and spread it out evenly. Cook over low heat, without stirring, for about 5 minutes or until the omelette is set around the edges but still soft in the centre. Lift the edge of the omelette gently with a knife to check the colour of the base – it should be golden brown.

Transfer to the oven and bake for about 5 minutes or until puffed up, set and lightly browned.

Make a shallow cut down the centre of the omelette and spoon the cheese and herb mixture down the cut. Scatter over the chive flowers, then fold the omelette over in half. Slide on to a plate and serve.

Spinach Custard with Tomato Sauce

Vegetable-based custards were often made with rich cream and cheese from the spotlessly clean Shaker dairies and fresh eggs from the hen house.

4 SERVINGS

700 g/1½ lb fresh spinach, stalks removed
170 g/6 oz creamy soft cheese or cottage cheese
250 ml/8 fl oz single cream
2 eggs
1 egg yolk
1 tablespoon chopped fresh tarragon
salt and pepper

FOR THE TOMATO SAUCE

700 g/1½ lb ripe plum-type tomatoes, peeled and chopped
15 g/½ oz butter
2 teaspoons tomato paste
½–1 teaspoon caster sugar
a few drops of Tabasco sauce (optional)

First make the tomato sauce. Put the tomatoes and butter in a heavy saucepan and simmer for about 20 minutes or until very soft and reduced, stirring occasionally. Stir in the tomato paste and sugar to taste. Add Tabasco sauce if desired and season with salt and pepper. Set aside.

Preheat the oven to 170°C/325°F/Gas 3.

Wash the spinach leaves thoroughly. Put the damp leaves in a large pan. Cover and steam until wilted, then uncover and simmer rapidly, stirring, until all the spinach is tender. Drain in a colander. When the spinach is cool enough to handle, squeeze out excess liquid. Chop the spinach coarsely.

Combine the creamy cheese or cottage cheese, cream, eggs, egg yolk and tarragon in a food processor. Work until smoothly blended. Add the spinach and season with

'Shakers,' or 'Believers,' enjoy the products of nature, with which they are amply supplied, and use all the comforts and conveniences which the fruits of their industry permit. They live not in luxury, but in comfort; not in extravagance but in sufficiency...An evidence that their daily life is far from being austere, is afforded by their records of mortality, which prove a greater longevity among the Shakers than any other class of people.

FROM *THE SHAKER*, DECEMBER, 1871

MUSHROOM AND RICE CAKES

At a time when city dwellers ate steak and pie for breakfast and lots of greasy food, the Shakers were advocating plain wholesome food – plenty of fruit and vegetables and whole grain flours for bread.

4 SERVINGS

30 g/1 oz butter
225 g/8 oz mushrooms, chopped
300 g/10 oz cooked rice, white or brown
260 g/9 oz mashed potatoes
4 tablespoons (10 g/⅓ oz) chopped fresh parsley
½ teaspoon grated lemon zest
salt and pepper
2 eggs
flour
fine cream cracker crumbs or toasted breadcrumbs
oil for frying

Melt the butter in a heavy frying pan. Add the mushrooms and cook until they are wilted, then continue cooking until the excess liquid has evaporated. Leave to cool.

Combine the mushrooms, rice and potatoes in a bowl. Add the parsley and lemon zest and season with salt and pepper. Lightly beat one of the eggs and add to the bowl. Mix the ingredients together thoroughly.

With well floured hands, shape the mushroom and rice mixture into eight cakes. Lightly beat the remaining egg. Dip the floured cakes in the beaten egg, then coat with crumbs, patting them on gently. Refrigerate for 20–30 minutes to set the coating.

Heat about 1.25 cm/½ inch of oil in a heavy frying pan and fry the cakes until they are a rich golden brown and crisp on both sides. Drain on paper towels and serve hot.

COOK'S NOTE The mashed potatoes should be quite dry in texture.

salt and pepper. Process for a few seconds to mix well.

Pour the spinach mixture into a lightly buttered 1 litre/1⅔ pint baking dish. Bake for 30–35 minutes or until set. Just before serving, warm the tomato sauce. Serve the spinach custard hot, with the sauce.

ELDRESS BERTHA LINDSAY AND SISTERS GOING TO BLACKSMITH ORCHARD
TO PICK APPLES, CANTERBURY SHAKER VILLAGE

BAKED STUFFED ACORN SQUASH

Not all Shakers wanted to follow a vegetarian diet, so tables were divided to allow those following the 'bloodless' diet to eat separately from those eating a 'regular' diet. However, the delicious meatless dishes devised by the kitchen Sisters would have been appealing to both.

4 SERVINGS

4 acorn squash or other small winter squash or
pumpkins, each weighing 450–525 g/1–1¼ lb
30 g/1 oz butter
½ Spanish onion, chopped
8 plump tenderized prunes, stoned and chopped
2 tart eating apples, peeled, cored and chopped
4 tablespoons pressed apple juice
¼ teaspoon ground ginger
salt and pepper
60 g/2 oz butternuts or walnuts, chopped

Preheat the oven to 200°C/400°F/Gas 6.

Cut the squash in half and scoop out the seeds and fibres. Arrange the squash halves, cut side down, in a shallow baking tin. Pour a little water into the tin. Bake the squash for 25–30 minutes or until just tender when pierced with a knife.

Meanwhile, melt the butter in a heavy saucepan, add the onion and cook until soft and golden. Stir in the prunes, apples, apple juice and ginger. Season with salt and pepper. Bring to the boil and simmer for 2 minutes. Remove from the heat and stir in the nuts. Set aside.

Turn the squash over. Season with salt and pepper. Fill the central hollows with the apple and prune mixture, packing it down and doming the top slightly. Return to the oven and bake for about 15 minutes or until the filling is hot and lightly browned. Serve hot.

FRIED CORNMEAL MUSH WITH COURGETTES

The cornmeal ground by the Shakers from their dry maize would have been much more nutritious than that made commercially today because it would have contained the whole grain. It would also have required more cooking to make mush, which was once a mainstay of American breakfasts.

4 SERVINGS

750 ml/1¼ pints water
1 teaspoon salt
125 g/4½ oz yellow cornmeal
15 g/½ oz butter plus more for frying
1 tablespoon vegetable oil
700–800 g/1½–1¾ lb courgettes, thinly sliced
1 tablespoon chopped fresh thyme
2 tablespoons chopped fresh marjoram
salt and pepper
tomato sauce (page 72, Spinach Custard), warmed

Put the water and salt in a saucepan and bring to the boil. Gradually rain in the cornmeal, stirring constantly. Cook, stirring, until very thick and bubbly.

Pour the cornmeal mush into a buttered 23 cm/9 inch square tin. Leave to cool, then refrigerate overnight to set.

The next day, cut the mush into squares or other shapes. Set aside.

Heat the butter with the oil in a heavy frying pan. Add the courgettes. Cook over moderate heat for 8–10 minutes or until just tender, stirring occasionally. Stir in the herbs and season with salt and pepper. Remove from the heat and keep warm.

Fry the squares of cornmeal mush in hot butter until golden brown on both sides. Serve topped with the courgettes and tomato sauce.

COOK'S NOTE If using dried thyme and oregano, add when frying the courgettes.

CHAPTER FOUR

SIDE DISHES

Both fresh and dried vegetables received simple treatment – often cooked in cream, a method that produces delicious results, as well as steamed or simmered in very little water. Shaker Sisters preferred to cook vegetables unpeeled if possible. Fresh salads, made from greens from the kitchen garden as well as those gathered from the wild, were originally dressed with a strong vinegar mixture sweetened with molasses.

CREAMED POTATOES

Cooking in cream was a very popular way of preparing vegetables. Original Shaker recipes would no doubt have used cream alone or very creamy milk.

4 SERVINGS

450 g/1 lb medium-size boiling potatoes
30 g/1 oz butter
250 ml/8 fl oz milk
125 ml/4 fl oz whipping cream
salt and pepper

Put the unpeeled potatoes in a pan of salted water, bring to the boil and simmer for 10 minutes. Drain. When the potatoes are cool enough to handle, peel them and cut into 1.25 cm/½ inch slices.

Melt the butter in a large heavy non-stick frying pan. Stir in the milk and cream and heat until bubbles appear round the edge. Season with salt and pepper. Add the potato slices to the pan, arranging them in one layer if possible. Reduce the heat so the liquid is simmering very gently, then leave to cook for about 1 hour or until the potatoes are very tender and have absorbed almost all the liquid. Move the potato slices gently from time to time during the cooking so they don't stick to the bottom of the pan. Serve hot.

FRIED TOMATOES

This is based on a recipe that appeared in *The Manifesto* in September, 1880. It is simple but very good.

4–6 SERVINGS

450 g/1 lb ripe but firm tomatoes
flour
grated nutmeg
salt and pepper
bacon fat or butter for frying

Cut out the core from each tomato, then cut into 1.25 cm/ $^1\!/_2$ inch thick slices. Mix flour with nutmeg, salt and pepper on a plate. Dip the tomato slices in the seasoned flour to coat lightly.

Heat bacon fat or butter in a heavy frying pan until very hot. Add the tomato slices and fry until lightly browned on both sides. Serve hot.

BAKED SQUASH

The large and immaculate kitchen gardens provided a wealth of produce, and vegetables and fruits were planted in rotation so that the growing season could be prolonged. In Shaker seed catalogues, an astonishing variety of vegetable seeds was offered, which included at least six kinds of squash.

6 SERVINGS

1.35 kg/3 lb butternut squash, halved
3–4 tablespoons pure maple syrup
30 g/1 oz butter
a large pinch of grated nutmeg
salt and pepper

Preheat the oven to 200°C/400°F/Gas 6.
Scoop out the seeds and fibres from the squash halves.

Put the pieces, cut side down, on a lightly oiled baking sheet. Bake for 1 hour or until soft and collapsed. Leave the squash to cool slightly, then scrape the flesh from the skin. Put the flesh in a food processor.

Add the maple syrup, butter and nutmeg to the squash. Season with salt and pepper. Process until smooth.

Turn the squash mixture into a buttered baking dish. Reheat in a 180°C/350°F/Gas 4 oven for about 15 minutes. Serve hot.

COOK'S NOTE You can also use pumpkin or other winter squash, allowing for weight of skin and seeds, or sweet potatoes.

CUCUMBERS IN CREAM

The idea of cooking cucumber may seem odd, but as one Believer wrote in *The Manifesto*: '...The cucumber is one of the most valuable vegetables we raise...Even when they have become too old to be served as salad and too tough for pickling, it is then that the cucumber is at its best for cooking.'

4–6 SERVINGS

2 cucumbers
30 g/1 oz butter
$^1\!/_2$ teaspoon caster sugar
salt and pepper
125 ml/4 fl oz whipping cream
1 tablespoon chopped fresh dill

Peel the cucumbers, then cut them lengthways in half. With the tip of a teaspoon, scrape out the central seeds. Cut across into 1.25 cm/$^1\!/_2$ inch pieces.

Melt the butter in a heavy frying pan. Add the cucumber pieces and sprinkle with the sugar. Season with salt and pepper. Sauté for 4–5 minutes, stirring.

Add the cream and bring to the boil, stirring well. Stir in the dill and serve.

GLAZED CARROTS

Although Believers were encouraged to grow lemon trees 'within doors', most lemons had to be bought from the World: this was one item the kitchen Sisters could not do without, whether to use as a seasoning or to make beverages and pie fillings.

4 SERVINGS

30 g/1 oz butter
450 g/1 lb carrots (about 10), thinly sliced
4 tablespoons pressed apple juice or dry cider
1 tablespoon light soft brown sugar
1 teaspoon lemon juice
salt and pepper

Melt the butter in a wide heavy saucepan. Add the carrots and apple juice. Cover and cook for 5 minutes, stirring occasionally.

Stir in the sugar and lemon juice. Season with salt and pepper. Cook uncovered until the liquid is almost all evaporated and the carrots are glazed and tender, stirring occasionally.

GREEN BEANS WITH BACON

When it was common practice for American cooks to boil vegetables in a lot of water for a long time, Shaker Sisters preferred steaming or cooking in very little water.

4–6 SERVINGS

6 smoked streaky bacon rashers, rind removed, chopped
a knob of butter
450 g/1 lb French beans, trimmed
4 tablespoons chicken stock or water
2 teaspoons chopped fresh marjoram
a pinch of sugar
4 tablespoons whipping cream
salt and pepper

Fry the bacon with the butter in a heavy frying pan until browned. Remove with a slotted spoon and drain on paper towels. Pour all but a thin film of fat from the pan.

Add the beans to the pan and pour in the stock or water. Add the marjoram and sugar. Bring to the boil, then cover and cook over moderately low heat for about 5 minutes or until the beans are just tender, stirring occasionally.

Uncover and stir in the cream. Season with salt and pepper. Bring back to the boil. Stir in the bacon. Simmer for 1 minute, then serve.

OVERLEAF: CLOCKWISE FROM LEFT: GREEN BEANS WITH BACON, GLAZED CARROTS, BEETROOT IN HONEY

POTATO CAKES WITH ROSEMARY

The humble potato was transformed in the hands of the creative Shaker Sisters, into salads, pies, soups, stews, stuffings, hash, breads, griddle cakes and side dishes.

6 SERVINGS

750 g/1 lb 10 oz mashed potatoes
1 egg
1½ tablespoons finely chopped fresh rosemary
salt and pepper
about 170 g/6 oz plain flour
butter for frying

Put the potatoes in a bowl, add the egg and beat until smoothly blended. Mix in the rosemary. Season with salt and pepper.

With floured hands, divide the potato mixture into 12 equal portions. Shape each into a cake about 1.25 cm/ ½ inch thick, reflouring your hands as necessary and, finally, coating each cake lightly with flour.

Heat butter in a heavy frying pan. Add the potato cakes and fry over moderate heat until golden brown on both sides, pressing to flatten them slightly. Serve hot.

COOK'S NOTE You can add fried onion to the potato mixture or use other herbs.

BEETROOT IN HONEY

In the late eighteenth century, honey, maple sugar and molasses were the commonly used sweeteners, and the Shakers produced both honey and maple sugar for their own use and to sell to the World.

4 SERVINGS

450 g/1 lb small raw beetroot
15 g/½ oz butter
3 tablespoons cider vinegar
about 3 tablespoons water
85 g/3 oz liquid honey
¼ teaspoon grated orange zest
salt and pepper

Trim and peel the beetroot, then cut them into thin slices. Melt the butter in a wide heavy pan and add the beetroot, vinegar and water. Bring to the boil, then cover and cook over a low heat until the beetroot are tender, stirring occasionally. Add a little more water if necessary.

Stir in the honey and orange zest and season with salt and pepper. Simmer, uncovered, to evaporate any excess liquid.

SLOW-BAKED BEANS

The Shakers made great quantities of baked beans, both to eat themselves and to sell to the World, often directly from the back of a truck, in nearby towns and cities. During a ban on pork, butter was used instead of salt pork to give richness.

8 OR MORE SERVINGS

450 g/1 lb dried white beans such as haricot beans,
soaked overnight
1 onion, peeled
115 g/4 oz salt pork or green bacon, cut into chunks
85 g/3 oz molasses or treacle
4 tablespoons (80 g/scant 3 oz) pure maple syrup
2 tablespoons cider vinegar
1 tablespoon dry mustard
salt and pepper

Drain the beans and put them in a saucepan. Cover with fresh cold water. Bring to the boil and boil for 10 minutes, then drain. Return the beans to the pan, cover with fresh water and bring to the boil. Reduce the heat and simmer gently for 1–1½ hours or until the beans are very tender. (Be sure they are thoroughly cooked at this stage because they won't soften any more once mixed with the remaining ingredients.)

Drain the beans in a colander set in a bowl; reserve the liquid.

Preheat the oven to 150°C/300°F/Gas 2.

Put the whole onion in the bottom of an earthenware bean pot or other deep casserole and add the beans and salt pork or bacon. Mix the remaining ingredients with 375 ml/12 fl oz of the reserved bean liquid and pour into the pot. Stir to mix. The beans should almost be covered with liquid, so add more of the reserved cooking liquid if necessary.

Cover the pot and bake the beans for 3½ hours. Stir from time to time and add a little more water if the beans seem to be drying out. Uncover and bake for a further 30 minutes, stirring occasionally. When done the beans should be a rich brown and the liquid thick. Discard the onion before serving.

GREEN CORN FRITTERS

When sweetcorn was eaten fresh, it was called 'green', meaning immature, because the most widely grown varieties of maize were dried to grind into meal or for other uses.

MAKES ABOUT 12

4–6 ears tender green (young) sweetcorn
2 eggs, beaten
30 g/1 oz butter, melted, plus more for frying
45 g/1½ oz plain flour
¼ teaspoon caster sugar
salt and pepper

Pull the green leaves and silk from the sweetcorn. With a sharp knife, cut the kernels from the cobs. Roughly chop the kernels. Or, grate off the kernels. You want about 450 g/1 lb.

Combine the eggs, melted butter, flour and sugar in a bowl. Beat together until smooth. Add the sweetcorn and season with salt and pepper.

Melt some butter in a heavy frying pan. Drop heaping spoonfuls of the sweetcorn mixture into the hot butter and flatten them slightly. Fry over moderate heat for 2–3 minutes on each side or until golden brown. Serve the fritters hot.

OVERLEAF: SLOW-BAKED BEANS (LEFT), STEAMED BROWN BREAD

HOME-MADE NOODLES

Home-made noodles were a popular alternative to pota-toes. They were often cooked in vegetable water ('pot liquor') to give them more flavour.

4 SERVINGS

280 g/10 oz plain flour
60 g/2 oz strong plain flour
½ teaspoon salt
30 g/1 oz soft butter
2 egg yolks
about 5 tablespoons water
cornmeal or polenta

TO FINISH

butter
chopped fresh chives

Sift the flours and salt into a bowl. Make a well in the centre and put in the butter, egg yolks and water. With your fingertips, mix together the butter, yolks and water, then gradually mix in the flour to make a dough. Add more water if necessary. Knead until the dough is smooth and firm.

Divide the dough into three or four portions. On a lightly floured surface, roll out each piece of dough as thinly as possible. Hang the sheets of dough over the back of a chair or over a clean broom handle and leave to dry for 15–20 minutes.

Roll up each sheet of dough loosely, like a Swiss roll, and cut across into 2 cm/¾ inch slices. Unroll these noodles and toss them with a little cornmeal or polenta.

Bring a large pot of salted water to the boil. Drop in the noodles. Bring the water back to the boil and cook for 5 minutes or until the noodles are just tender (bite one to check). Drain and return to the pot. Add butter and chives and toss to coat the noodles. Serve immediately.

CABBAGE SALAD

There are many recipes for cabbage salad, or cole slaw, in Shaker manuscripts, as well as for cooking cabbage in cream and braising it with apples. Cabbage was also the essential accompaniment for 'corned' or salt beef.

8 SERVINGS

1 medium-size green cabbage
1 large carrot, shredded
1 green apple, cored and grated
1–2 teaspoons caraway seeds

FOR THE BOILED DRESSING

1 teaspoon dry mustard
70 g/2½ oz caster sugar
1 tablespoon plain flour
½ teaspoon salt
125 ml/4 fl oz cider vinegar
2 eggs
125 ml/4 fl oz water
30 g/1 oz butter
2–4 tablespoons soured cream or plain yogurt

First make the dressing. Combine the mustard, sugar, flour, salt and vinegar in a small bowl and whisk to mix. Put the eggs and water in the top of a double boiler and whisk together. Whisk in the mustard mixture. Set over simmering water and cook for about 10 minutes or until the dressing thickens, stirring frequently. Remove from the heat and stir in the butter. Leave to cool, then stir in the soured cream or yogurt.

Cut the cabbage into quarters and cut out the core. Slice across the quarters into fine shreds.

Combine the cabbage, carrot, apple and dressing in a large bowl. Toss well together. Add the caraway seeds and mix again. Cover and refrigerate until ready to serve.

COOK'S NOTE The boiled dressing can also be used to dress potato or other vegetable salads.

GREEN BEAN SALAD

We might view the nasturtium flowers as a pretty decoration for this salad, but the Shakers' principles of thriftiness and plainness meant the flowers would not have been grown just to be admired. The original recipe added nasturtium pods too, which the Shakers also pickled.

4–6 SERVINGS

340 g/12 oz bobby beans or other green beans
1 large bunch of spring onions, thinly sliced
¼ Iceberg lettuce, shredded
2 teaspoons chopped fresh summer savory
a handful of nasturtium leaves, shredded if large
a handful of nasturtium flowers

FOR THE DRESSING

5 tablespoons vegetable or olive oil
2 tablespoons lemon juice
½ teaspoon prepared mustard, preferably Dijon
salt and pepper

Drop the beans into a saucepan of boiling salted water and cook until just tender but still with a crunch. Drain and refresh under cold running water. Pat the beans dry with paper towels and put into a bowl.

Put the dressing ingredients in a small bowl and whisk together (or shake them together in a jar). Pour the dressing over the warm beans and toss together. Leave the beans to cool completely.

Just before serving, add the spring onions, lettuce, savory and nasturtium leaves. Toss well. Scatter the nasturtium flowers on top and serve immediately.

CUCUMBER AND MINT SALAD

Shaker Sisters used herbs liberally in cooking. The freshness of mint could enliven a dish of vegetables, a salad or a beverage, or flavour a sauce or pudding.

4–6 SERVINGS

1 cucumber
a handful of fresh mint leaves
1½ teaspoons caster sugar
3 tablespoons cider vinegar
125 ml/4 fl oz soured cream
salt and pepper
3–4 spring onions, white part only, thinly sliced

Cut the cucumber across into thin slices.

Reserve 3 or 4 mint leaves; put the rest in a large bowl. Add the sugar to the bowl. Press and mash the mint leaves with a spoon to release the oils into the sugar. Add the vinegar and stir to dissolve the sugar. Remove the mint leaves, pressing and squeezing them to extract all the liquid, and discard.

Add the soured cream to the bowl and stir to mix with the mint vinegar. Season with salt and pepper. Add the cucumber slices and spring onions and toss to coat with the dressing. Cover and chill for about 45 minutes.

Before serving, shred the reserved mint leaves and scatter them over the salad.

OVERLEAF: GREEN BEAN SALAD (LEFT), CUCUMBER AND MINT SALAD

CHAPTER FIVE

BREADS AND BAKING

In Shaker diaries and recipe collections there are many hints and tips for making breads, rolls and muffins. The kitchen Sisters had to bake enough to provide a variety of breads at every meal for their Families of 50 or more people. Their revolving ovens could bake dozens of loaves at a time. Cakes were weekly treats, at Sunday supper.

MAPLE WHEATEN BREAD

Shakers were amongst the first to advocate the use of whole grain flour in baking.

MAKES 2 LOAVES

scant 1 tablespoon dried yeast (7 g/ ¼ oz)
250 ml/8 fl oz warm water (40–43°C/105–110°F)
3 tablespoons pure maple syrup, warmed
about 280 g/10 oz strong plain white flour
1½ teaspoons salt
450 g/1 lb strong wholemeal flour
250 ml/8 fl oz warm milk
30 g/1 oz butter, melted and cooled, plus extra for glazing

Put the yeast, 4 tablespoons warm water and ½ table-spoon of the maple syrup in a small bowl. Leave to soak for 1 minute, then whisk with a fork to dissolve the yeast.

Sift the white flour and salt into a large bowl. Add the wholemeal flour and stir to mix. Make a well in the centre and pour in the yeast mixture, milk, butter and remaining 2½ tablespoons maple syrup and 175 ml/6 fl oz water. Mix the ingredients in the well, then gradually draw in the flour. Mix to a soft but not sticky dough, adding more white flour if the dough feels too wet or a little more liquid if the dough will not come together.

Turn the dough on to a floured surface and knead for about 10 minutes or until smooth and elastic. Shape the dough into a ball. Put it in a lightly buttered bowl and rotate so that the surface of the ball is greased all over. Cover and leave to rise in a warm, draught-free place for about 1½ hours or until doubled in bulk.

Gently knock back the dough to deflate it, and fold the sides to the centre. Knead again for 2–3 minutes. Divide the dough in half and shape into loaves, tucking the ends under. Put into two greased 21 or 23 cm/8½ or 9 inch loaf tins. Leave to rise in a warm place for 30–45 minutes.

Preheat the oven to 200°C/400°F/Gas 6. Brush the

Wheat should be used in whole, and ground coarse...No flour should be ground so fine that the teeth have no office left them to perform...Indigestion would be as rare in America as it is in Ireland, with its potato; Scotland, with its oatmeal; Germany, with its cabbage, or in England with its good, strong common sense...beginning with the Queen, who, during some part of her reign, prohibited absolutely the whole royal household from using a single loaf of bread made from superfine ground and bolted wheat flour.

FROM *SHAKER AND SHAKERESS*, NOVEMBER, 1873

loaves with melted butter, then bake for 45–50 minutes or until well risen and browned. Tip the loaves out of their tins and tap the base with your knuckles: the bread should sound hollow, like a drum. Cool on a wire rack.

SWEET POTATO BREAD

Bread ovens in Shaker kitchens could accommodate dozens of loaf tins at a time, and the range of recipes used by the Sisters ensured that those loaves provided a wonderful variety.

MAKES 1 LARGE ROUND LOAF

scant 1 tablespoon dried yeast (7 g/¼ oz)
175 ml/6 fl oz warm water (40–43°C/105–110°F)
3 tablespoons flower blossom honey
about 200 g/7 oz plain flour
about 700 g/1 lb 9 oz strong plain flour
1½ teaspoons salt
1½ teaspoons grated orange zest
255 g/9 oz mashed or puréed sweet potato
175 ml/6 fl oz warm milk
30 g/1 oz butter, melted and cooled
beaten egg to glaze

Put the yeast, 4 tablespoons warm water and 1 tablespoon of the honey in a small bowl. Leave to soak for 1 minute, then whisk with a fork to dissolve the yeast.

Sift the flours and salt into a large bowl. Add the orange zest and stir to mix. Make a well in the centre and add the yeast mixture, sweet potato, milk, butter and remaining honey and water. Mix the ingredients in the well, then gradually draw in the flour. Continue mixing to make a soft but not sticky dough, adding more flour if the dough feels too soft and wet or a little more liquid if the dough will not come together.

Turn the dough on to a floured surface and knead for about 10 minutes or until smooth and elastic. Shape the dough into a ball. Put it in a lightly buttered bowl and rotate so that the surface of the ball is greased all over. Cover and leave to rise in a warm, draught-free place for 1–1½ hours or until doubled in bulk.

Gently knock back the dough to deflate it, and fold the sides to the centre. Knead again for 2–3 minutes. Shape the dough into a large round loaf and set it on a lightly greased baking sheet. Leave to rise in a warm place for 30–45 minutes.

Preheat the oven to 200°C/400°F/Gas 6. Brush the loaf with beaten egg, then bake for 45–50 minutes or until well risen and browned. Transfer to a wire rack to cool.

COOK'S NOTE You can also divide the dough and bake in loaf tins or cut into three, shape into ropes and plait together.

SCENTED LEAF ROLLS

Bread rolls of all kinds appeared on the table for 12 o'clock dinner, to accompany meat and vegetables.

MAKES ABOUT 42

scant 1 tablespoon dried yeast (7 g/¼ oz)
250 ml/8 fl oz warm water (40–43°C/105–110°F)
1½ tablespoons caster sugar
about 200 g/7 oz plain flour
about 700 g/1 lb 9 oz strong plain flour
1½ teaspoons salt
350 ml/12 fl oz warm milk
55 g/2 oz butter, melted and cooled, plus extra for dipping
fresh herb leaves such as lemon balm, marjoram, thyme or lovage, washed and dried

Put the yeast, 4 tablespoons warm water and ½ tablespoon of the sugar in a small bowl. Leave to soak for 1 minute, then whisk with a fork to dissolve the yeast.

Sift the flours, salt and remaining sugar into a large bowl. Make a well in the centre and add the yeast mixture, milk, butter and remaining water. Mix the ingredients in the well, then gradually draw in the flour. Continue mixing to make a soft but not sticky dough, adding more flour if the dough feels too soft and wet or a little more liquid if the dough will not come together.

Turn the dough on to a floured surface and knead for

OVERLEAF: SCENTED LEAF ROLLS (LEFT), MAPLE WHEATEN BREAD

about 10 minutes or until smooth and elastic. Shape the dough into a ball. Put it in a lightly buttered bowl and rotate so that the surface of the ball is greased all over. Cover and leave to rise in a warm, draught-free place for 1–1½ hours or until doubled in bulk.

Gently knock back the dough to deflate it, and fold the sides to the centre. Knead again for 2–3 minutes. Pull off pieces of dough to make balls about 5 cm/2 inches in diameter. Make a hole into the centre of each ball with your finger, press in a single herb leaf or a few small ones and bring the dough around to seal. Roll into a neat ball again and smooth with your thumbs, working from the top to the base and tucking the ends under. Dip the balls in melted butter, then arrange in one or more baking tins; the balls should just touch each other. Leave to rise in a warm place for 30–45 minutes.

Preheat the oven to 200°C/400°F/Gas 6. Bake the rolls for 20–25 minutes or until well risen and golden brown. Transfer to a wire rack to cool. Best served warm.

That bread is eaten at all tables in connection with other food, and the benefits resulting therefrom, are easily seen. It necessitates slow eating and thorough mastication, and would be a most excellent thing for Americans, who are in the habit of bolting their food in five or ten minutes, and then run to the doctor to complain of indigestion, or to the druggist for some pills. It would be much better if they would stay at the table at least half an hour, and attend to their digestion themselves, by eating proper things in a proper manner. This would also give the doctors and druggists an opportunity of earning their livelihood by some kind of honest work.

FROM *SHAKER AND SHAKERESS*, NOVEMBER, 1873

HERB AND CHEESE BREAD

The Shaker Sisters made buttermilk, cream of all kinds, cheeses and butter and used these dairy products generously in their cooking. An extract from a journal dated November 30, 1843, quoted in *Gleanings from Old Shaker Journals*, compiled by Clara Endicott Sears, reads: 'We weigh our cheese. Have made twenty-nine hundred pounds.'

MAKES 1 LOAF

200 g/7 oz plain flour
55 g/2 oz strong plain flour
2 teaspoons baking powder
½ teaspoon bicarbonate of soda
½ teaspoon salt
80 g/2½ oz strong wholemeal flour
100 g/3½ oz mature Cheddar cheese or other firm well-flavoured cheese, finely grated
1½ teaspoons crumbled dried sage
1 teaspoon dried dill
about 300 ml/½ pint buttermilk

Preheat the oven to 180°C/350°F/Gas 4.

Sift the white flours, baking powder, bicarbonate of soda and salt into a bowl. Add the wholemeal flour, three-quarters of the cheese and the herbs and stir to mix. Add enough buttermilk to mix to a soft dough.

Form the dough gently into a bolster shape and put it in a buttered 21 × 11 cm/8½ × 4½ inch loaf tin. Sprinkle the remaining cheese over the top.

Bake for 50–60 minutes or until golden brown and a skewer inserted in the centre comes out clean. Leave to cool in the tin for a few minutes before turning out. Serve warm or cold.

COOK'S NOTE As an alternative to buttermilk you can use milk soured with 1½ teaspoons cream of tartar.

CORN BREAD

The original varieties of corn, or maize, were far less sweet than those we enjoy today, and were most often dried for storage, later to be ground into cornmeal or hominy as well as to provide cattle feed and dried cobs to burn as fuel. In early Shaker days, hundreds of pounds of maize were dried every year to sustain communities through the winter, and they perfected a means of drying maize that would keep it year round without any spoilage.

6–8 SERVINGS

130 g/4½ oz yellow cornmeal
115 g/4 oz plain flour
55 g/2 oz strong plain flour
1 tablespoon baking powder
¾ teaspoon salt
1 tablespoon caster sugar
2 eggs, beaten
250 ml/8 fl oz milk
85 g/3 oz butter
165 g/6 oz fresh sweetcorn kernels cut from the cob

Preheat the oven to 200°C/400°F/Gas 6.

Sift the cornmeal, flours, baking powder, salt and sugar into a bowl. Add the eggs and milk and mix to a smooth batter.

Put the butter in a 23 or 25 cm/9 or 10 inch cast iron frying pan with an ovenproof handle. Heat in the oven until the butter has melted. Tilt and rotate the pan to coat with butter, then pour the remaining butter into the batter. Add the sweetcorn and mix well.

Pour the sweetcorn mixture into the hot pan and return to the oven. Bake for 25–30 minutes or until set and golden brown.

Serve hot, cut into wedges.

COOK'S NOTE The mixture can also be baked in a 23 cm/9 inch round or square cake tin or in muffin tins or deep bun tins.

STEAMED BROWN BREAD

A traditional New England bread, often served with baked beans, this was still being sold by Shakers in New Hampshire in the 1930s.

MAKES 1 LOAF

60 g/2 oz rye flour
85 g/3 oz strong wholemeal flour
60 g/2 oz yellow cornmeal
½ teaspoon salt
1 teaspoon bicarbonate of soda
250 ml/8 fl oz buttermilk
115 g/4 oz molasses or treacle
75 g/2½ oz raisins

Thoroughly wash and dry a 450 g/1 lb coffee can (1 litre/1⅔ pint capacity). Butter it generously. Set a rack in the bottom of a large saucepan that is deep enough to accommodate the can, and add enough water to the pan to cover the rack. Bring to the boil.

Combine the rye flour, wholemeal flour, cornmeal, salt and bicarbonate of soda in a bowl. In another bowl, stir the buttermilk with the molasses until evenly blended. Add to the dry ingredients and mix well. Stir in the raisins.

Pour the mixture into the can. Cover the top tightly with foil and tie on with string. Set the can on the rack in the pan. Pour more boiling water into the pan so that the level is halfway up the can. Reduce the heat so the water is barely simmering, then cover the pan tightly and steam for about 2 hours. Top up with more boiling water as necessary. To test if the bread is cooked, insert a long wooden skewer into the centre: it should come out clean.

Remove the can from the saucepan and leave to cool for about 5 minutes, then turn out the bread on to a wire rack. Serve warm or cold.

WHIPPED CREAM BISCUITS

These wonderful light-textured scone-like 'biscuits' would have been usual fare on breakfast and supper tables.

MAKES 14–16

255 g/9 oz plain flour
85 g/3 oz strong plain flour
1 tablespoon baking powder
½ teaspoon salt
a pinch of sugar
300 ml/½ pint whipping cream
melted butter

Preheat the oven to 220°C/425°F/Gas 7.

Sift the flours, baking powder, salt and sugar into a bowl. In another bowl, whip the cream until it is thick but not stiff. Add to the dry ingredients and mix together thoroughly but lightly to make a soft dough.

Turn the dough on to a lightly floured surface and pat or roll out to 1.25 cm/½ inch thickness. Use a floured 5–6 cm/2–2½ inch cutter to cut out rounds (cut cleanly and don't twist the cutter). Arrange on an ungreased baking sheet and brush the tops with melted butter. Bake for 15 minutes or until risen and golden brown. Serve hot.

ROSEWATER SPONGE CAKE

Flavouring essences as we know them today were not readily obtainable, so most cooks used rosewater or citrus zest for flavouring cakes, pies and puddings. Many distilled their own rosewater – particularly so the Shakers, who made very large quantities both to use and to sell.

8 SERVINGS

4 eggs, separated
a pinch of cream of tartar
150 g/5 oz caster sugar
1 tablespoon rosewater
130 g/4½ oz plain flour
icing sugar to sprinkle

Preheat the oven to 180°C/350°F/Gas 4. Butter and flour a 23 cm/9 inch round cake tin and line the bottom with a disc of greaseproof paper.

In a large bowl beat the egg whites until frothy. Add the cream of tartar and continue beating until the whites will form soft peaks. Sprinkle in 2 tablespoons of the caster sugar and beat until the whites will form stiff peaks. Set aside.

In another bowl, beat the egg yolks until frothy. Add the remaining caster sugar and continue beating until the mixture is very thick and pale – if you lift out the beaters the mixture should trail back on to the surface in a ribbon that holds its shape. Add the rosewater.

Sift the flour over the surface of the egg yolk mixture and fold it in gently but thoroughly. Add a large spoonful of the egg whites and mix in, then fold in the remainder. Pour the mixture into the prepared tin. Bake for 35–40 minutes or until risen and lightly browned. Leave to cool in the tin.

Turn out the cake. Dust the top with a little sifted icing sugar before serving. Best eaten the day of baking.

PREVIOUS PAGES: WHIPPED CREAM BISCUITS (LEFT), HERB AND CHEESE BREAD

MOTHER ANN'S BIRTHDAY CAKE

The birthday of the founder of the Shaker society was Februrary 29, but it was usually celebrated March 1 unless it was a leap year. The original recipe instructions were to beat the cake mixture with a handful of bruised peach twigs, '...which are filled with sap at this season of the year...This will impart a delicate peach flavor to the cake'.

MAKES A 2-LAYER CAKE

6 egg whites
a pinch of cream of tartar
300 g/10 oz caster sugar
225 g/8 oz soft butter
1 teaspoon pure vanilla essence
425 g/15 oz plain flour
1 tablespoon baking powder
175 ml/6 fl oz milk
225 g/8 oz peach jam

FOR THE BUTTERCREAM

420 g/15 oz icing sugar, sifted
135 g/4½ oz soft butter
1½ teaspoons pure vanilla essence
about 2 tablespoons half cream or milk

Preheat the oven to 180°C/350°F/Gas 4. Butter and flour two 20 or 21 cm/8 or 8½ inch round cake tins and line the bottom of each with a disc of greaseproof paper.

Beat the egg whites until frothy. Add the cream of tartar and continue beating until soft peaks will form. Gradually sprinkle 4 tablespoons of the sugar over the whites and beat until glossy and stiff peaks will form. Set aside.

In another bowl beat the butter with the remaining sugar and the vanilla essence until pale and very fluffy (the consistency of whipped cream). Sift together the flour and baking powder. Gradually add to the butter mixture alternately with the milk. Add a large spoonful of the egg whites and mix in to loosen the mixture, then fold in the remaining whites with a rubber spatula.

Divide the mixture equally between the prepared tins. Bake for about 30 minutes or until golden brown and a wooden skewer inserted in the centre comes out clean. Leave to cool.

When the cake layers are cold, spread one with the peach jam and set the second layer on top.

To make the buttercream, gradually beat the sugar into the soft butter to make a pale, fluffy mixture. Beat in the vanilla and enough cream to make a spreadable consistency. Spread the buttercream over the top and side of the cake.

GINGERBREAD

Sometimes maple sap was boiled to a concentrated dark brown syrup that resembled molasses, and this was then used to sweeten gingerbread and baked beans in place of molasses.

MAKES A 23 CM/9 INCH SQUARE CAKE

310 g/11 oz plain flour
115 g/4 oz strong plain flour
1½ teaspoons bicarbonate of soda
¼ teaspoon salt
2 teaspoons ground ginger
1 teaspoon ground cinnamon
¼ teaspoon ground cloves
55 g/2 oz white vegetable fat
55 g/2 oz soft butter
115 g/4 oz dark soft brown sugar
250 g/scant 9 oz molasses or treacle
2 eggs
250 ml/8 fl oz hot water

Preheat the oven to 180°C/350°F/Gas 4. Butter a 23 cm/ 9 inch square cake tin and line the bottom with grease-proof paper.

Sift the flours, bicarbonate of soda, salt and spices into a bowl. Set aside.

In another bowl, cream the vegetable fat with the butter. Add the sugar and beat until well blended and creamy. Beat in the molasses and then the eggs. Gradually add the flour mixture alternately with the water, beating well after each addition.

Pour the mixture into the prepared tin. Bake for 35–40 minutes or until firm and a wooden skewer inserted in the centre comes out clean. Set the tin on a wire rack to cool. Serve warm or at room temperature.

SPICY APPLESAUCE CAKE

Shaker applesauce was much loved both by the Believers and by those in the World who bought it. It was made in quantity and put up in wooden firkins or glass jars, to be ready for use in spicy cakes such as this one.

MAKES A 23 CM/9 INCH SQUARE CAKE

255 g/9 oz plain flour
85 g/3 oz strong plain flour
1 teaspoon baking powder
½ teaspoon bicarbonate of soda
½ teaspoon salt
225 g/8 oz light soft brown sugar
100 g/3½ oz caster sugar
1 teaspoon ground cinnamon
½ teaspoon ground allspice
½ teaspoon grated nutmeg
¼ teaspoon ground cloves
115 g/4 oz soft butter
2 eggs, lightly beaten
125 ml/4 fl oz milk
415 g/14 oz applesauce (page 139)

Preheat the oven to 180°C/350°F/Gas 4. Grease and flour a 23 cm/9 inch square cake tin. Line the bottom with greaseproof paper.

Sift the flours, baking powder, bicarbonate of soda, salt, sugars and spices into a bowl. Add the butter and beat to mix. Beat in the eggs and milk until the batter is evenly blended. Mix in the applesauce, keeping the pieces of apple whole.

Pour the mixture into the prepared tin and spread out evenly. Bake for 40–45 minutes or until firm and a wooden skewer inserted in the centre comes out clean.

Serve warm or at room temperature, plain or topped with whipped cream.

COMB HONEY CAKE

The Shakers kept beehives and honey was much used as a sweetener in place of sugar. Natural raw honey has much more flavour than the purified store-bought product, as well as a positively heady aroma.

MAKES A 20 CM/8 INCH SQUARE CAKE

325 g/11½ oz plain flour
100 g/3½ oz strong plain flour
1 teaspoon baking powder
½ teaspoon bicarbonate of soda
¼ teaspoon salt
½ teaspoon ground cinnamon
¼ teaspoon grated nutmeg
425 g/15 oz runny honey from the comb plus extra for drizzling
170 g/6 oz butter
3 eggs, lightly beaten
4 tablespoons milk
30 g/1 oz flaked almonds

Preheat the oven to 170°C/325°F/Gas 3. Butter and flour a 20 cm/8 inch square cake tin and line the bottom with greaseproof paper.

Sift the flours, baking powder, bicarbonate of soda, salt and spices into a bowl. Set aside.

Warm the honey with the butter just until the butter has melted. Remove from the heat and beat in the eggs and milk. Gradually add to the dry ingredients, beating well after each addition.

Pour into the prepared tin and scatter the almonds over the surface. Bake for 1–1¼ hours or until browned and a wooden skewer inserted in the centre comes out clean. Cover with foil if the cake is browning too much.

Remove the cake from the oven and prick the surface all over with a skewer or fork. Drizzle some extra honey evenly over the surface. Leave to cool in the tin set on a wire rack.

FRUIT AND NUT LOAF

Fruits from Shaker orchards, particularly apples, were dried for winter storage, and then used in breads, pies, puddings and stuffing for poultry.

MAKES A 21 CM/8½ INCH LOAF CAKE

80 g/2¾ oz dried peaches or apricots, chopped
45 g/1½ oz dried apples, chopped
90 g/3 oz raisins
225 g/8 oz light soft brown sugar
30 g/1 oz butter
250 ml/8 fl oz pressed apple juice
255 g/9 oz plain flour
85 g/3 oz strong plain flour
2 teaspoons baking powder
¼ teaspoon salt
1 teaspoon grated orange zest
2 eggs, lightly beaten
90 g/3 oz butternuts, walnuts or pecan nuts, chopped

Combine the peaches, apples and raisins in a small saucepan with the sugar, butter and apple juice. Bring to the boil, stirring to dissolve the sugar, then remove from the heat and leave to cool.

Preheat the oven to 180°C/350°F/Gas 4. Butter and flour a 21 × 11 cm/8½ × 4½ inch loaf tin and line the bottom with greaseproof paper.

Sift the flours, baking powder and salt into a bowl. Add the fruit and apple juice mixture, the orange zest, eggs and nuts and mix together quickly and evenly.

Pour into the prepared tin. Bake for about 1 hour or until risen and golden brown and a wooden skewer inserted in the centre comes out clean. Cover the top with foil if it is browning too much. Cool in the tin.

OVERLEAF: PECAN MUFFINS (LEFT), COMB HONEY CAKE

PECAN MUFFINS

Nut trees abounded in Shaker orchards – walnut, butter-nut and hickory. The delicious nut of the hickory, the pecan, takes its name from Native American languages.

MAKES 12–18 (ACCORDING TO THE TINS USED)

255 g/9 oz plain flour
85 g/3 oz strong plain flour
2 teaspoons baking powder
½ teaspoon salt
115 g/4 oz light soft brown sugar
1 teaspoon ground cinnamon
½ teaspoon grated lemon zest
250 ml/8 fl oz milk
2 eggs
55 g/2 oz butter, melted and cooled
65 g/2¼ oz pecan nuts, chopped

Preheat the oven to 200°C/400°F/Gas 6.

Sift the flours, baking powder, salt, sugar and cinnamon into a bowl. Stir in the lemon zest. Combine the milk, eggs and butter and mix well. Add to the dry ingredients together with the pecans. Stir just until blended, leaving lumps in the dough.

Spoon into buttered muffin tins, or deep bun tins, filling them two-thirds full. Bake for 20–25 minutes or until risen and golden brown. Leave to cool in the tins for about 1 minute, then turn out on to a wire rack.

SUGAR COOKIES

Before the sugar tariffs were lifted in the United States, in the 1880s, white sugar was expensive, so frugal cooks used molasses, honey and maple sugar or syrup instead. With their beehives and acres of maple trees, the Shakers could be self-sufficient in these sweeteners.

MAKES ABOUT 36

170 g/6 oz soft butter
200 g/7 oz granulated maple sugar or caster sugar
plus extra for sprinkling
1 teaspoon grated lemon zest
2 eggs
340 g/12 oz plain flour
170 g/6 oz strong plain flour
½ teaspoon salt
¼ teaspoon grated nutmeg

Beat the butter with the sugar and lemon zest until well blended and creamy. Beat in the eggs. Sift the flours with the salt and nutmeg and gradually beat into the butter mixture. Add more flour if necessary to make a dough that can be rolled out. Gather into a ball, wrap and chill for about 20 minutes.

Preheat the oven to 190°C/375°F/Gas 5.

Roll out the dough to about 1.25 cm/½ inch thickness. Cut into rounds or other shapes with biscuit cutters. Place on lightly greased baking sheets and sprinkle the cookies lightly with sugar. Alternatively, take large walnut-size pieces of dough and shape into balls. Arrange on the baking sheets, leaving plenty of space between each ball. Butter the base of a large glass, dip it in sugar and use to flatten the balls (one greasing will do, but dip the glass in sugar each time).

Bake for 8–10 minutes or until the cookies are lightly golden brown around the edge and just firm to the touch. Cool on a wire rack.

CINNAMON SOURED CREAM COOKIES

MAKES ABOUT 40

115 g/4 oz soft butter
225 g/8 oz light soft brown sugar
1 egg
125 ml/4 fl oz soured cream
½ teaspoon bicarbonate of soda
310 g/11 oz plain flour
115 g/4 oz strong plain flour
1 teaspoon baking powder
¼ teaspoon salt
1½ teaspoons ground cinnamon

Beat the butter with the sugar until well blended and creamy. Beat in the egg. Mix together the soured cream and bicarbonate of soda and add to the butter mixture. Sift the flours, baking powder, salt and cinnamon into a bowl, then add to the butter mixture. Beat well to make a soft dough. It will be sticky, so cover and chill for about 30 minutes (if the kitchen is hot, you may need to chill the dough a little longer).

Preheat the oven to 190°C/375°F/Gas 5.

Take large walnut-size pieces of dough and roll into balls. Arrange on lightly greased baking sheets, leaving space for spreading. Flatten the balls with a floured fork. Bake for 10–15 minutes or until golden brown and still slightly soft in the centre.

Leave to cool for 1–2 minutes on the baking sheets, then transfer to wire racks to cool completely.

PECAN BALLS

MAKES 30–36

255 g/9 oz plain flour
85 g/3 oz strong plain flour
½ teaspoon salt
225 g/8 oz soft butter
55 g/2 oz icing sugar, sifted, plus extra for dusting
1 teaspoon pure vanilla essence
115 g/4 oz pecan nuts, finely chopped

Preheat the oven to 180°C/350°F/Gas 4.

Sift the flours with the salt and set aside. Beat the butter with the sugar and vanilla until well blended and creamy. Gradually beat in the flour, then mix in the pecans.

Take pieces of dough and roll into large walnut-size balls. Arrange on ungreased baking sheets. Bake for 15–20 minutes or until set and very lightly browned.

Leave to cool for 1 minute on the baking sheets, then transfer to wire racks. While still warm, dust with icing sugar. Store in an airtight tin with more icing sugar.

OVERLEAF: SUGAR COOKIES (LEFT), CRANBERRY OAT COOKIES

A MODERN VERSION OF A SHAKER KITCHEN, SHOWING THE SIMPLE DESIGNS AND SUBTLE COLOURS
TYPICAL OF SHAKER DECORATION

MOLASSES COOKIES

Molasses, which is what remains after sugar cane juice is boiled until it crystallizes, was the most widely used sweetener in America in the nineteenth century. In addition to sweetening cookies, cakes, pie fillings, quick breads and so on, it was added to meat dishes and to hot and cold drinks. Shaker switchel, or 'haying water', was a refreshing cold drink made from water, ginger, sugar or maple syrup, and molasses.

MAKES ABOUT 36

115 g/4 oz soft butter
100 g/3½ oz caster sugar
165 g/scant 6 oz molasses or treacle
1 egg
255 g/9 oz plain flour
85 g/3 oz strong plain flour
2 teaspoons bicarbonate of soda
¼ teaspoon salt
1 teaspoon ground ginger
½ teaspoon grated nutmeg
¼ teaspoon ground cloves

Preheat the oven to 190°C/375°F/Gas 5.

Beat the butter with the sugar and molasses until well blended and creamy. Beat in the egg. Sift the flours, bicarbonate of soda, salt and spices into another bowl. Gradually add to the molasses mixture, beating well after each addition.

Drop heaped tablespoons of the dough on to lightly greased baking sheets, leaving space for spreading. Bake for 10–12 minutes or until just firm in the centre. Leave to cool on the sheets for a few seconds, then transfer to wire racks to cool completely.

CRANBERRY OAT COOKIES

Cranberry vines were cultivated on Shaker farms, and the berries were used fresh or they were bottled or dried. When dried, they often replaced the more expensive raisins in baked goods and puddings.

MAKES ABOUT 24

85 g/3 oz plain flour
45 g/1½ oz strong plain flour
½ teaspoon bicarbonate of soda
½ teaspoon salt
½ teaspoon ground cinnamon
115 g/4 oz soft butter
115 g/4 oz light soft brown sugar
50 g/1¾ oz caster sugar
1 egg
½ teaspoon pure vanilla essence
80 g/2½ oz porridge oats
80 g/2½ oz dried unsweetened cranberries

Preheat the oven to 180°C/350°F/Gas 4.

Sift the flours, bicarbonate of soda, salt and cinnamon into a bowl. Set aside. In another bowl, beat the butter with the sugars until well blended and creamy. Add the egg and vanilla essence and beat well. Beat in the sifted dry ingredients until smooth. Stir in the porridge oats and cranberries.

Drop heaped tablespoonfuls of the dough on to lightly greased baking sheets, leaving room for spreading. Flatten each cookie slightly. Bake for 15 minutes or until lightly browned. Leave to cool on the baking sheets for about 1 minute, then transfer to a wire rack to cool completely.

CHAPTER SIX

DESSERTS, PIES AND CANDIES

At one time, pies were served at all meals, but as the nineteenth century ended it became more common to have them just at dinner and supper. Apple pie was a favourite, traditionally flavoured with rosewater, and was often eaten with cheese. Simple puddings, often based on rich milk or cream, were eaten at dinner too, while candies were occasional pleasures.

Apple and Blackberry Batter Pudding

Seasonal fruits, rich cream and eggs, and freshly ground spices were used to make simple desserts. The kitchen Sisters laboured to produce meals for their Families that would satisfy both the body's hunger and the spirit – in keeping with the Shaker mission to 'create a heaven on earth'.

6–8 SERVINGS

4 green apples such as Granny Smith's, peeled, cored
and chopped
115 g/4 oz light soft brown sugar
½ teaspoon ground cinnamon
¼ teaspoon ground cloves
¼ teaspoon grated nutmeg
350 g/12 oz blackberries
2 eggs
100 g/3½ oz caster sugar
85 g/3 oz plain flour
175 ml/6 fl oz whipping or single cream
1 teaspoon pure vanilla essence

Preheat the oven to 180°C/350°F/Gas 4.

Combine the apples, brown sugar and spices and toss to mix. Put into a buttered shallow 1.5 litre/2⅓ pint baking dish and scatter the blackberries evenly on top.

In a bowl, lightly whisk the eggs with the caster sugar until the sugar has dissolved. Add the flour and mix well, then stir in the cream and vanilla essence until smooth. Pour this batter evenly over the fruit.

Bake for about 40 minutes or until the apples are tender and the top of the pudding is set and golden brown. Serve warm.

COOK'S NOTE This pudding could also be made with plums and apricots.

Baked Rice Pudding

Simple, thrifty puddings were much loved, and were always prepared with care, using the best ingredients.

6 SERVINGS

750 ml/1¼ pints milk
500 ml/16 fl oz cream or half cream
1 teaspoon pure vanilla essence
100 g/3½ oz caster sugar
a pinch of salt
100 g/3½ oz short-grain pudding rice
¼-½ teaspoon grated nutmeg
boiled cider syrup (page 135) to serve

Preheat the oven to 150°C/300°F/Gas 2.

Combine all the ingredients except the cider syrup in a buttered shallow baking dish and stir to mix. Bake for 30 minutes, then stir the pudding. Bake for a further 15 minutes, then stir again. Bake for another 15 minutes and stir, then continue baking, without stirring, for 1½ hours or until the pudding is creamy and the top is golden brown. Cover the top with foil if it is browning too much.

Serve hot or at room temperature, with cider syrup.

COOK'S NOTE Use any combination of milk and cream you like, according to how rich a pudding you want.

BREAD PUDDING

Many Shaker recipes use 'stale' bread. This was usually an extra loaf baked and kept a day. It might then be dried in the oven and coarsely ground by rolling to use as a crumb coating.

8 SERVINGS

600 ml/1 pint milk
55 g/2 oz butter
100 g/3½ oz caster sugar
1 teaspoon grated lemon zest
1 teaspoon pure vanilla essence
½ teaspoon ground cinnamon
200 g/7 oz slightly stale white bread without crusts,
cut into cubes
40 g/1½ oz dried cherries
3 eggs, beaten
30 g/1 oz toasted pecan nuts, chopped

FOR THE SAUCE

225 g/8 oz dark soft brown sugar
115 g/4 oz butter
4 tablespoons whipping cream

Combine the milk, butter and sugar in a heavy saucepan and heat, stirring to dissolve the sugar. Pour into a bowl. Stir in the lemon zest, vanilla and cinnamon. Add the bread cubes and cherries and stir to mix. Leave to soak for 20 minutes.

Preheat the oven to 180°C/350°F/Gas 4.

Stir the eggs into the bread mixture. Add the pecans. Pour into a buttered shallow baking dish. Bake for about 40 minutes or until set and golden brown on top.

Meanwhile, prepare the sauce. Combine the sugar and butter in a heavy saucepan and heat gently, stirring, to melt the butter and dissolve the sugar. Bring to the boil, then stir in the cream. Remove from the heat.

Serve the pudding hot, with the sauce.

COOK'S NOTE Use bread with a good firm texture. If you prefer, serve the pudding with whipped cream or with soured cream and pure maple syrup.

BLUEBERRY CRISP

Blueberry bushes produced abundant fruit that was used in desserts such as cobblers and crisps or brown betties, which are similar to crumbles, as well as in pies and muffins.

4–6 SERVINGS

800 g/1¾ lb blueberries
1–2 tablespoons granulated sugar
1 teaspoon grated orange zest

FOR THE TOPPING

130 g/4½ oz plain flour
165 g/5½ oz light soft brown sugar
85 g/3 oz butter, cut into pieces
40 g/scant 1½ oz porridge oats
½ teaspoon ground cinnamon

Preheat the oven to 180°C/350°F/Gas 4.

Combine the blueberries, sugar and orange zest and toss to mix. Put into a buttered shallow baking dish.

To make the topping, combine the flour, sugar and butter in a food processor and work just until the mixture resembles very coarse crumbs. (Turn the machine on and off a few times and take care not to process too finely.) Add the oats and cinnamon and process for a few more seconds to blend.

Spread the topping mixture evenly over the fruit and pat down gently with your fingertips. Bake for 35–40 minutes or until the top is lightly browned and crisp. Serve warm, with whipped cream or vanilla ice cream.

OVERLEAF: BLUEBERRY CRISP (LEFT), STRAWBERRY SHORTCAKE

CITRUS SPONGE PUDDING WITH CHERRY SAUCE

6 SERVINGS

55 g/2 oz soft butter
130 g/4½ oz caster sugar
1 tablespoon grated orange zest
1 teaspoon grated lemon zest
3 eggs, separated
55 g/2 oz plain flour
175 ml/6 fl oz milk
125 ml/4 fl oz orange juice
2 tablespoons lemon juice
a pinch of cream of tartar

FOR THE SAUCE

200 g/7 oz fresh sweet cherries, stoned
125 ml/4 fl oz water
4 tablespoons orange juice
100 g/3½ oz sugar

Preheat the oven to 180°C/350°F/Gas 4.

Beat the butter with the sugar, orange zest and lemon zest until very light and fluffy. Beat in the egg yolks and flour, then mix in the milk and juices. In another bowl, beat the egg whites until frothy. Add the cream of tartar and continue beating until soft peaks form. Add a large spoonful of the egg whites to the citrus mixture and beat in gently, then fold in the remaining whites.

Pour into a buttered 1 litre/1⅔ pint baking dish. Set the dish in a roasting tin containing hot water and bake for 40–45 minutes or until the pudding is golden brown and set and springs back when lightly pressed in the centre.

Meanwhile, make the sauce. Combine the cherries, water, orange juice and sugar in a saucepan and heat, stirring to dissolve the sugar. Bring to the boil and simmer for 1 minute. With a slotted spoon remove the cherries from the pan and reserve. Continue boiling

the liquid until it is reduced and syrupy. Return the cherries to the liquid and stir to mix. Set aside.

Serve the pudding hot with the warm cherry sauce.

STRAWBERRY SHORTCAKE

The large strawberry fields yielded basket upon basket of juicy, aromatic fruit, to make delicious jams and desserts. Strawberry shortcake was an early summer treat for Shaker Families.

6 SERVINGS

700 g/1½ lb strawberries, hulled and sliced
100 g/3½ oz caster sugar
300 ml/½ pint whipping cream
1 teaspoon pure vanilla essence

FOR THE SHORTCAKE

255 g/9 oz plain flour
85 g/3 oz strong plain flour
2½ teaspoons baking powder
4 tablespoons caster sugar
45 g/1½ oz butter
55 g/2 oz white vegetable fat
5-6 tablespoons half cream
1 egg, beaten

Put the strawberries in a bowl and sprinkle with half of the sugar. Toss gently. Cover and refrigerate.

Preheat the oven to 220°C/425°F/Gas 7.

To make the shortcake, sift the flours, baking powder and sugar into a bowl. Rub in the butter and vegetable fat until the mixture resembles fine crumbs. Add the cream and egg and mix quickly to a soft dough.

Roll or pat out the dough to just over 1.25 cm/½ inch thick and cut out six 7.5 cm/3 inch rounds (take care not to twist the cutter). Set the rounds on an ungreased baking sheet, arranging them so they are nearly touching. Bake for about 15 minutes or until well risen and golden brown. Transfer to a wire rack and leave to cool slightly.

Meanwhile, whip the cream until beginning to thicken. Add the remaining sugar and the vanilla essence and continue whipping until thick.

Split the warm shortcake rounds horizontally in half. Fill with the whipped cream and strawberries and serve immediately.

APPLE DUMPLINGS

To make maple sugar, the Shakers boiled the gallons of syrup they tapped from their trees until it was much reduced and concentrated. This syrup was beaten until it became creamy-brown in colour, and it was poured into moulds to set. The resulting maple sugar had a smooth texture (not crystalline like commercial granulated maple sugar), and it was shaved off to use in pies, cakes, cookies, puddings and vegetable dishes.

4 SERVINGS

4 tart green apples such as Granny Smith's, peeled
4 tablespoons granulated or shaved maple sugar
4 tablespoons whipping cream
30 g/1 oz butter, cut into small pieces
175 ml/6 fl oz pressed apple juice
125 ml/4 fl oz (160 g/5½ oz) pure maple syrup

FOR THE PASTRY

225 g/8 oz plain flour
¼ teaspoon salt
115–140 g/4–5 oz cold butter, or half butter and half white vegetable fat, cut into pieces
3–4 tablespoons cold water

First make the pastry dough. Put the flour and salt in the food processor and turn the machine on briefly to blend.

Add the butter and process until the mixture resembles coarse crumbs, turning the machine on and off several times. Add enough water to bind the ingredients (the mixture should still look crumbly). Turn on to the work surface and mix briefly with your hands to make a smooth dough. Gather into a ball, wrap and refrigerate for 20 minutes.

Preheat the oven to 190°C/375°F/Gas 5.

Roll out the pastry dough thinly. Cut into four squares, each large enough to wrap an apple.

Using a small melon baller, remove the cores from the apples, working from the tops and keeping them whole. Do not cut all the way through. Put an apple in the centre of each square of dough. Fill the hollow in each apple with maple sugar and cream and put the butter on top. Moisten the edges of the dough squares with water. Bring the corners of each square up over the top of the apple and press to seal; fold over and press all the edges to seal. Prick around the top of each dumpling with a fork to make a few steam vent holes.

Set the dumplings in a shallow baking tin and pour the apple juice and maple syrup round them. Bake for 45 minutes or until the apples are tender and the pastry is golden brown. Baste with the cider and syrup mixture every 15 minutes.

Serve the dumplings hot, with the pan juices.

COOK'S NOTE You can substitute soft light brown sugar for maple sugar.

SUMMER BERRY PUDDING

Fruits of all kinds were cultivated in Shaker fields and orchards, and the Brothers were always experimenting – grafting and testing new varieties. Kitchen Sisters had fresh fruits available almost all year round.

6 SERVINGS

900 g/2 lb mixed berries, such as raspberries, blackberries, blueberries, strawberries and red or blackcurrants
100 g/3½ oz caster sugar
2–4 tablespoons blackberry cordial (page 142) or other fruit liqueur
8–12 slices of white bread, cut 1.25 cm/½ inch thick, crusts trimmed

If using strawberries that are large, cut them in half or quarters so they are about the same size as the other berries. Put the berries in a heavy saucepan with the sugar. Cook over a low heat, stirring gently to dissolve the sugar, until the juices start to run from the fruit. Remove the pan from the heat and stir in the blackberry cordial.

Butter a 1.2 litre/2 pint mould and line the bottom with a disc of greaseproof paper. Layer the bread and fruit in the mould, cutting the slices of bread to fit neatly and fill the gaps. Press each layer of fruit and bread firmly (without squashing the fruit too much). Start and finish with bread (make three or four layers of bread, according to taste). Moisten the top layer of bread with the fruit juices. Set a saucer or small plate on the bread and weight down (with a can of food, for example). Refrigerate overnight.

Turn out the pudding to serve, with cream.

BAKED PEACHES

The Shakers preferred to cook fruits and vegetables without peeling them, so that nothing would be wasted.

4 SERVINGS

soft butter
55 g/2 oz granulated maple sugar or light soft brown sugar
4 ripe but firm peaches

Preheat the oven to 190°C/375°F/Gas 5.

Rub some soft butter over the bottom of a baking dish just large enough to accommodate 8 peach halves. Sprinkle the sugar evenly over the butter.

If you prefer, peel the peaches. Cut the peaches in half and remove the stones. Arrange the halves cut side down in the baking dish. Bake for 10 minutes.

Turn the peach halves over and continue baking for 5 minutes.

Serve hot or at room temperature, with ice cream, whipped cream or gingerbread (page 104).

ICED LEMON CREAM

The Shakers at North Union built an icehouse in 1874 to store the ice they cut from their lakes in winter. The ice could be kept for months, and then used in the summer to chill drinks, store food and freeze ice cream in the dairy.

MAKES JUST OVER 1 LITRE/1²/₃ PINTS

1 tablespoon grated lemon zest
150 ml/¼ pint fresh lemon juice
400 g/14 oz sugar
4 tablespoons water
750 ml/1¼ pints whipping cream
250 ml/8 fl oz half cream or milk

Combine the lemon zest and juice, sugar and water in a saucepan and bring to the boil, stirring to dissolve the sugar. Remove from the heat and leave to cool.

Mix together the cream and half cream or milk in a bowl. Strain in the lemon mixture and stir to mix. Pour into an ice cream machine (hand-cranked or electric) and freeze until firm.

BERRY WATER ICE

Among many Shaker kitchen inventions was a motorized ice cream freezer.

MAKES ABOUT 500 ML/16 FL OZ

450 g/1 lb strawberries, raspberries or blackberries
150–200 g/5–7 oz caster sugar
125 ml/4 fl oz water
1–2 tablespoons lemon juice

Purée the berries with 150 g/5 oz sugar in a food processor or blender. Add the water and 1 tablespoon lemon juice and process again until very smooth and the sugar has dissolved. Pass the purée through a fine nylon sieve, pressing firmly with a rubber spatula. Taste and add more sugar and/or lemon juice: the mixture should be highly flavoured.

In cooking, and the general labor of the dining-room and kitchen, the sisters take turns; a certain number, sufficient to make the work light, serving a month at a time...Their diet is simple but efficient.

CHARLES NORDHOFF
THE COMMUNISTIC SOCIETIES OF THE UNITED STATES, 1875

Pour into an ice cream machine (hand-cranked or electric) and freeze until firm. Or, still freeze in a container, whisking several times to prevent large ice crystals forming.

ROSEWATER ICE CREAM

At one time, it was forbidden for flowers to be grown simply for their beauty and scent – they had to have a function, culinary or medicinal. Roses were cultivated only for the making of rosewater, which was used as a flavouring as well as to cure fever. These strict rules were relaxed in the late nineteenth century.

MAKES ABOUT 1 LITRE/1²/₃ PINTS

500 ml/16 fl oz whipping cream
250 ml/8 fl oz milk
150 g/5 oz caster sugar
6 egg yolks
250 ml/8 fl oz single cream
1 tablespoon rosewater or more to taste

Put 250 ml/8 fl oz of the whipping cream and the milk in a heavy saucepan and heat until bubbles appear round the edge. Add the sugar and heat almost to boiling point, stirring to dissolve the sugar.

Lightly beat the egg yolks in a bowl. Slowly add the hot cream mixture to the yolks, stirring constantly. Pour back into the pan (or into the top of a double boiler, if you prefer) and cook over moderately low heat, stirring, until the custard thickens enough to coat the spoon thinly. Do not boil.

Strain the custard into a bowl or jug and stir in the remaining cream and rosewater to taste (the mixture should be highly flavoured). Pour into an ice cream machine (hand-cranked or electric) and freeze until firm.

COOKS' NOTE For a less rich ice cream use 500 ml/16 fl oz each cream and milk.

OVERLEAF: ROSEWATER ICE CREAM (LEFT), MAPLE PECAN FUDGE

RHUBARB AND STRAWBERRY PIE

Shaker Sisters were always baking pies, with fillings chosen according to the season: soft fruits in spring and summer; squash, sweet potatoes and cranberries in the autumn; mincemeat and other preserved fruits in winter. A revolving oven, designed by Eldress Emeline Hart at Canterbury, New Hampshire, in 1876, could accommodate dozens of pies or loaves of bread at the same time.

8 OR MORE SERVINGS

450 g/1 lb rhubarb, cut into 2.5 cm/1 inch pieces
400 g/14 oz strawberries, hulled and sliced
2 tablespoons plain flour or instant tapioca
100 g/3½ oz caster sugar plus extra for sprinkling
115 g/4 oz light soft brown sugar
15 g/½ oz butter, cut into small flakes
single cream

FOR THE PASTRY

280 g/10 oz plain flour
½ teaspoon salt
140 g/5 oz cold butter, or half butter and half white vegetable fat, cut into pieces
1 egg yolk lightly beaten with 3–4 tablespoons cold water
soft butter

To make the pastry dough, put the flour and salt in the food processor and turn the machine on briefly to blend. Add the butter and process until the mixture resembles coarse crumbs, turning the machine on and off several times. Add the egg yolk mixture to bind the ingredients (the mixture should still look crumbly). Turn on to the work surface and mix briefly with your hands to make a smooth dough. Gather into a ball, wrap and refrigerate for 20 minutes.

Preheat the oven to 190°C/375°F/Gas 5.

Divide the pastry dough into two portions, one larger than the other. Roll out the larger portion and use to line a 23 cm/9 inch pie plate that is about 5 cm/2 inches deep. Brush a film of soft butter over the bottom of the pastry case.

Combine the rhubarb, strawberries, flour or tapioca and sugars in a bowl and toss gently to mix well. Pour into the pastry case and spread out evenly, doming the fruit slightly in the centre. Dot with the flakes of butter. Roll out the remaining dough, cut into strips and use to make a lattice top. Brush the strips lightly with cream and sprinkle them with caster sugar.

Bake the pie for about 45 minutes or until the pastry is golden brown and the fruit filling is juicy and tender. Cover the pastry edge with foil if it is browning too much. Set the pie plate on a wire rack to cool. Serve directly from the pie plate.

COOK'S NOTE If the strawberries are very ripe and the rhubarb is likely to be juicy, you may need to use a little more flour or tapioca.

APPLE PIE

Apple pie, with its traditional flavouring of rosewater, was a Shaker favourite, and according to the season the pie would be made with fresh or dried apples. The orchards were very large, and huge quantities of apples were cut and dried every fall. Even the children helped in the preparation.

8 OR MORE SERVINGS

pastry for a double-crust pie (page 127, Lemon Pie)
900 g/2 lb tart eating apples, peeled, cored and thinly sliced
150 g/5 oz caster sugar (or more according to the sweetness of the apples) plus extra for sprinkling
2 tablespoons whipping cream
1 tablespoon rosewater

Preheat the oven to 190°C/375°F/Gas 5.

Divide the pastry dough into two portions, one slightly larger than the other. Roll out the larger portion and use to line a 23 cm/9 inch pie plate that is about 5 cm/2 inches deep.

Combine the apple slices, sugar, cream and rosewater in a bowl and mix well together. Tip into the pastry case and spread out evenly. Roll out the remaining dough for the top crust and crimp the edges to seal. Cut a few slits in the top crust as steam vent holes. Brush the crust lightly with water and sprinkle with sugar.

Bake the pie for about 45 minutes or until the pastry is golden brown and the apples are tender. Cover the pastry edge with foil if it is browning too much. Set the pie plate on a wire rack to cool. Serve directly from the pie plate.

LEMON PIE

Rich lemon pie like this was traditionally made by the Ohio and Kentucky Shakers, but recipes for lemon pies of all kinds appear in the diaries and handwritten cook-books of all Shaker communities.

8 OR MORE SERVINGS

2 large or 3 medium-size juicy unwaxed lemons,
well scrubbed
about 400 g/14 oz caster sugar
soft butter
4 eggs

FOR THE PASTRY

280 g/10 oz self-raising flour
½ teaspoon salt
85 g/3 oz cold butter, cut into pieces
85 g/3 oz cold white vegetable fat, cut into pieces
1 egg yolk lightly beaten with 3 tablespoons cold
water

Cut the lemons into paper-thin slices, then quarter the slices if liked. Remove any seeds and discard the end slices. Layer the lemon slices in a bowl, sprinkling with 400 g/14 oz of sugar. Cover the bowl and leave to stand for several hours, or overnight if more convenient.

To make the pastry dough, put the flour and salt in the food processor and turn the machine on briefly to blend. Add the butter and vegetable fat and process until the mixture resembles coarse crumbs, turning the machine on and off several times. Add the egg yolk mixture to bind the ingredients (the mixture should still look crumbly). Turn on to the work surface and mix briefly with your hands to make a smooth dough. Gather into a ball, wrap and refrigerate for 20 minutes.

Preheat the oven to 190°C/375°F/Gas 5.

Divide the dough into two portions, one slightly larger than the other. Roll out the larger portion and use to line a 23 cm/9 inch pie plate about 5 cm/2 inches deep. Brush the bottom of the pastry case with a film of soft butter.

Lift the lemon slices out of the bowl and layer them in the pastry case. Sprinkle with a little more sugar if liked. Add the eggs to the sugary lemon juice in the bowl and beat until well blended. Pour over the lemon slices. Roll out the remaining dough for the top crust and crimp the edges to seal. Cut a few slits in the top crust.

Bake the pie for 40–45 minutes or until the pastry is golden brown. Cover the pastry edge with foil if it is browning too much. Set the pie plate on a wire rack to cool. Serve directly from the pie plate.

OVERLEAF: LEMON PIE

PEACH AND APRICOT LEATHER

The delicious sweetmeat called fruit leather was one of many ways to use up dried fruits. Leathers could be sweetened with sugar or honey.

MAKES ABOUT 300 G/10 OZ

115 g/4 oz dried apricots
115 g/4 oz dried peaches
375 ml/12 fl oz water
100 g/3½ oz caster sugar
icing sugar

Combine the apricots, peaches and water in a saucepan. Bring to the boil, then remove from the heat. Cover and leave to soak overnight.

The next day, bring back to the boil and simmer, covered, for 30–35 minutes or until the fruit is very soft and pulpy. Leave to cool slightly, then purée in a blender or food processor. Add the caster sugar and blend until completely dissolved. Return the purée to the pan and continue cooking, uncovered, over low heat for 10–20 minutes or until the fruit mixture is very thick and excess liquid has evaporated. When done, a spoon drawn through the mixture will leave a clear channel on the bottom of the pan. Stir frequently during cooking to be sure the mixture doesn't stick. Remove from the heat and leave to cool slightly.

Turn on to 2 large baking sheets lined with greaseproof paper and spread out evenly with a rubber spatula to very thin sheets. Leave to cool and dry; when ready the leather should no longer feel tacky to the touch.

With scissors, cut the leather into strips and dust with sifted icing sugar to prevent the strips sticking together. Store in an airtight tin.

COOK'S NOTE Drying can take 1–2 days depending on the moisture in the air. You can speed things by drying in a very low oven.

MAPLE PECAN FUDGE

In the early spring, when the snow is still on the ground, the sap starts to rise in the maple tree; then it is time for 'sugaring off' to make maple syrup, an event greatly anticipated in Shaker communities.

MAKES ABOUT 80 PIECES

310 g/11 oz sugar
425 g/15 oz pure maple syrup
250 ml/8 fl oz whipping cream
¼ teaspoon salt
¼ teaspoon cream of tartar
225 g/8 oz pecans or other nuts, coarsely chopped
1 teaspoon pure vanilla essence

Butter the sides of a heavy deep saucepan. Put the sugar, maple syrup, cream, salt and cream of tartar in the pan and heat, stirring to dissolve the sugar. Once dissolved, stop stirring and bring to the boil. Boil to the soft ball stage (115°C/238°F on a sugar thermometer).

Meanwhile, spread the nuts evenly in a buttered 23 cm/9 inch square tin.

Remove the saucepan from the heat and allow the bubbles to subside, then stir in the vanilla essence. Leave to cool to 43°C/110°F, then beat with a wooden spoon until the mixture starts to thicken and look creamy. Quickly pour into the buttered tin over the nuts (do not scrape out the saucepan). Leave to cool, then cut into 2.5 cm/1 inch squares. Best freshly made.

COOK'S NOTE Unless you are an experienced fudge maker, it is best to use a sugar thermometer.

MOLASSES CREAM TAFFY

In the late nineteenth century, parties called taffy pulls were very popular amongst young people. The Shakers, too, enjoyed the fun of stretching the candy, and they invented a taffy hook to help.

MAKES ABOUT 450 G/1 LB

325 g/11½ oz molasses or treacle
200 g/7 oz sugar
2 teaspoons vinegar
125 ml/4 fl oz single cream
30 g/1 oz butter, cut into small flakes
icing sugar

Butter the sides of a heavy saucepan. Combine the molasses, sugar and vinegar in the pan and heat gently, stirring to dissolve the sugar. Once the sugar has dissolved, stop stirring, increase the heat and bring the mixture to the boil. Boil to the soft ball stage (115°C/238°F on a sugar thermometer).

Gradually stir in the cream, then add the butter, a few pieces at a time. Bring back to the boil, without stirring, and boil over moderate heat to just over the soft crack stage (130–132°C/265–270°F).

Pour the hot syrup slowly into a lightly buttered roasting tin (do not scrape the saucepan). Leave to cool for 2–3 minutes, then begin working the syrup with a candy or pastry scraper, turning and pushing it into a mass in the centre of the tin. When it is cool enough to handle, start working the taffy with buttered fingers (not your whole hand), pulling it out as far as it will stretch and then folding it back on itself. Continue the pulling and folding until the taffy starts to firm and is no longer sticky. Then add twisting to the pulling and folding. The taffy is ready when it is opaque and firm yet elastic.

Pull it into a twisted rope about 2.5 cm/1 inch thick and let it fall on to greaseproof paper. Snip into pieces with buttered scissors. When they are cool, toss the pieces of taffy in sifted icing sugar to prevent them sticking together and store in an airtight tin, or wrap them individually in greaseproof paper.

COOK'S NOTE Work with batches that you can comfortably hold. Try to pull the taffy in a cool place: if the room is warm and humid, the pulling can take up to 20 minutes.

SPRING WAS THE TIME TO FORM MAPLE SUGAR CANDIES, SHOWN HERE AT CANTERBURY SHAKER VILLAGE

CHAPTER SEVEN

PRESERVES, SAUCES AND BEVERAGES

Vast quantities of bottled and dried fruits and vegetables, plus pickles, relishes, jams and other preserves, were prepared throughout the growing season for the winter stores as well as to sell to the World. Applesauce, in particular, was made in such bulk that it was eaten at every meal. Apples were also pressed into cider, which was a favourite beverage together with fruit wines and herbal teas.

SWEETCORN RELISH

Pickles, relishes and sauces enlivened the simply prepared food on Shaker tables, and provided variety during the winter months.

MAKES ABOUT 1.5 LITRES/2⅓ PINTS

8 ears of sweetcorn
1 large onion, finely chopped
1 red pepper, seeded and diced
1 green pepper, seeded and diced
2 celery stalks, diced
½ small green cabbage (about 225 g/8 oz), finely chopped
200 g/7 oz sugar
300 ml/½ pint cider vinegar
125 ml/4 fl oz water
2 teaspoons mustard seeds
½ teaspoon turmeric
1½ teaspoons salt

Remove the green leaves and silk from the sweetcorn. With a sharp knife, cut the kernels from the cobs.

Put the sweetcorn kernels in a large non-reactive saucepan and add the remaining ingredients. Bring just to the boil, stirring to dissolve the sugar. Simmer gently for 30 minutes, stirring occasionally.

Pack into hot sterilized jars and cover. When cold, store in a cool dry place.

CRANBERRY CATSUP

Shaker cooks ground their own spices, using a mill or a mortar and pestle, so they were always fresh and fragrant.

MAKES ABOUT 1 LITRE/1⅔ PINTS

400 g/14 oz cranberries
1 onion, finely chopped
450 g/1 lb light soft brown sugar, or half white and half brown sugar
250 ml/8 fl oz cider vinegar
250 ml/8 fl oz water
1 teaspoon salt
½ teaspoon pepper
1 teaspoon ground allspice
½ teaspoon ground mace

Combine all the ingredients in a large non-reactive saucepan. Bring just to the boil, stirring to dissolve the sugar. Reduce the heat and simmer gently for about 45 minutes or until the cranberries are very tender and pulped.

Leave to cool slightly, then ladle into a food processor and work until quite smooth. Press through a sieve into a clean pan.

Bring the catsup back to the boil. If necessary, simmer until thickened to a catsup consistency, stirring occasionally. (Keep watching to be sure the catsup doesn't thicken too much and turn into a jam!)

Pack into hot sterilized bottles and seal.

SPICED PICKLED PEARS

It was common for each of the Families in a Shaker community to have its own fruit orchards, growing pears, peaches, apples, plums, cherries and quinces, according to climate.

400 g/14 oz sugar
600 ml/1 pint distilled white vinegar or half white
and half cider vinegar
600 ml/1 pint water
6 cinnamon sticks
2 tablespoons whole cloves
1 tablespoon black peppercorns
1.35 kg/3 lb small firm pears

Combine the sugar, vinegar and water in a large non-reactive saucepan. Add the spices. Bring to the boil, stirring to dissolve the sugar. Boil for 5 minutes. Remove from the heat.

Peel the pears. Core them from the base, using a melon baller or small knife, so that they stay whole. Add the pears to the spiced syrup as they are prepared.

Bring the syrup back to the boil, then reduce the heat and simmer until the pears are tender but still firm.

Remove the pears with a slotted spoon and pack into a hot sterilized jar that is just large enough to accommodate them. Boil the syrup until it is reduced to about 500 ml/16 fl oz. Strain the syrup. Add a few of the spices to the jar, then pour the syrup over the pears to fill the jar. Seal. When cold, store in a cool dark place.

COOK'S NOTE If you prefer, tie the spices in a muslin bag.

BOILED CIDER SYRUP

Shaker boiled cider was made by slowly boiling freshly pressed apple juice until it had reduced to about one-quarter of the original volume. It was used as a flavouring, and as a sweetener in place of sugar. (In the US, the term cider is used both for pressed apple juice and for its fermented alcoholic counterpart.)

MAKES ABOUT 375 ML/12 FL OZ

2 litres/3½ pints dry cider or pressed apple juice
1 cinnamon stick, broken in half
a few whole cloves
150–200 g/5–7 oz sugar

Put the cider and spices in a large wide pan and bring to the boil. Skim off the foam that rises to the surface. Boil the cider until it has reduced to about 500 ml/16 fl oz.

Add sugar to taste (according to the sweetness of the apples used to make the cider) and stir until it has dissolved. Continue boiling until the cider is just syrupy: take a little on a teaspoon, cool and tilt the spoon to see how the syrup runs.

Strain the syrup and pour it into a sterilized bottle.

COOK'S NOTE The spiced tart-sweet syrup can be served with desserts such as rice pudding, baked custard and bread pudding, and used to baste pork chops and gammon steaks.

OVERLEAF: CRANBERRY CATSUP (LEFT), APPLESAUCE

HERB VINEGARS

The early Shakers learned about wild herbs and roots from the Native Americans, and they transplanted both culinary and medicinal herbs to their gardens to cultivate. As a result Shaker Sisters had many different herbs available for cooking as well as to make teas and herbal medicines. In time, the selling of dried herbs became the chief source of income for many Shaker communities.

sprigs of fresh herbs, such as mint, tarragon,
rosemary, thyme, sage, basil, bay, fennel,
chives, marjoram or dill
mild white or cider vinegar
(use only white vinegar for mint)

Put the lightly crushed herb sprigs (one kind or a mixture) in a sterilized bottle. Warm the vinegar and pour it over the herbs. Seal and leave to stand for 2–3 weeks.

Strain the vinegar, pressing all liquid from the herbs. Discard the herbs. Put fresh herb sprigs in the bottle and pour in the vinegar. Seal again and keep in a cool dark place.

COOK'S NOTE If you prefer, use wine vinegar.

APPLE BUTTER

Applesauce and apple butter were made in quantity every autumn, and the Shaker-invented machine that peeled, cored and quartered or sliced apples no doubt made the job much faster and easier.

MAKES ABOUT 1 LITRE/1⅔ PINTS

1 litre/1⅔ pints pressed apple juice
1.35 kg/3 lb cooking apples, peeled, cored and
chopped
225 g/8 oz light soft brown sugar
225 g/8 oz dark soft brown sugar
2 teaspoons ground cinnamon
1 teaspoon ground allspice
1 teaspoon ground ginger

Put the apple juice in a large wide saucepan and bring to the boil. Boil until reduced to 250 ml/8 fl oz, skimming the surface occasionally.

Add the apples to the juice. Cover and simmer for 15–20 minutes or until the apples are very soft and pulpy.

Remove from the heat and mash the apples until smooth, or purée in a food processor or blender and return to the pan.

Add the sugars and spices and stir to dissolve the sugar. Simmer very gently for about 45 minutes or until very thick. When ready, you should be able to draw a spoon through the apple butter, leaving a clear channel on the bottom of the pan that slowly fills up. Stir frequently during cooking to prevent the apple butter from sticking to the pan, and partly cover the pan if necessary as the apple butter spatters a lot as it bubbles.

Ladle into hot sterilized jars and seal.

COOK'S NOTE Use well-flavoured tart apples.

APPLESAUCE

Shaker applesauce was traditionally made from boiled cider and from either fresh apples or soaked dried apples. The pieces of apple remained whole in the rich syrup. Applesauce was sold to the World for over 50 years.

MAKES ABOUT 1 LITRE/1⅔ PINTS

1.5 litres/2⅓ pints dry cider
900 g/2 lb tart eating apples, peeled, cored and sliced
sugar to taste, brown or white
lemon juice to taste

Pour the cider into a large wide saucepan and bring to the boil. Skim the foam from the surface. Boil until reduced to 375 ml/12 fl oz.

Add the apple slices, cover and simmer gently for about 10 minutes or until they are tender but still firm. With a slotted spoon, remove the apple slices. Pack into hot sterilized jars if you are intending to keep the applesauce; otherwise, transfer to a bowl.

Sweeten the cider to taste and boil until it is a little syrupy. Add a squeeze or two of lemon juice to sharpen the flavour, then pour the syrup over the apples. Serve warm or cold.

COOK'S NOTES If you prefer, substitute pressed apple juice for the cider. Depending on the apples used to make the cider or juice, and how sweet you like applesauce, you may not need much sugar. If you prefer a smooth applesauce, you can mash the apples before mixing in the syrupy cider.

A JAR LABEL SHOWING THE 'SHAKERS' MASTERY OF EYE-CATCHING DESIGN

Fragrant puffs of boiling fruit and spices emanated from the basement kitchen and filled the halls – perhaps they were making apple sauce that day. The odor suggested it.

WRITTEN BY A VISITOR TO SABBATHDAY LAKE IN 1910, QUOTED IN
THE FOUR SEASONS OF SHAKER LIFE BY GERARD C. WERTKIN

OVERLEAF: HERB VINEGARS

RASPBERRY SHRUB

The original shrubs, from colonial days, were fermented alcoholic drinks. In 1828 the Shaker central ministry forbade strong drink in all communities, and thereafter the much enjoyed cider had to be left to sour into vinegar.

MAKES 900 ML–1 LITRE/1½–1⅔ PINTS

600 g/1¼ lb raspberries
125 ml/4 fl oz mild cider vinegar
caster sugar
still or sparkling mineral water

Put the berries in a large non-reactive bowl and crush lightly with a fork or potato masher. Add the vinegar and stir to mix. Cover and leave to stand for 24 hours.

Strain the juice, rubbing as much of the pulp through the sieve as possible. Measure the juice. To each 250 ml/ 8 fl oz add 200 g/7 oz sugar. Put into a saucepan and heat, stirring to dissolve the sugar. Bring just to the boil.

Pour the syrup into hot sterilized bottles. Keep in the refrigerator and use within 3–4 weeks.

To serve, dilute one part syrup with three or four parts still or sparkling mineral water and pour into glasses over crushed ice.

COOK'S NOTE If you want to keep the raspberry syrup longer than 3–4 weeks, you can boil it before bottling; this will prevent it fermenting. However, boiling the syrup will lessen its very fresh flavour.

BLACKBERRY CORDIAL

Fruit cordials were prepared as medicinal drinks, and they were given to the sick and elderly.

MAKES ABOUT 750 ML/1¼ PINTS

750 g/1 lb 10 oz ripe blackberries
2 cinnamon sticks
1 teaspoon whole cloves
1 teaspoon whole allspice
about 200 g/7 oz sugar
250 ml/8 fl oz brandy

Purée the blackberries in a blender or food processor, then press the purée through a fine nylon sieve. Put the resulting blackberry juice in a saucepan and add the spices. Sweeten the juice with sugar to taste. Bring just to the boil, stirring to dissolve the sugar, then simmer gently for about 5 minutes.

Strain the blackberry syrup and leave to cool. When cold, stir in the brandy. Store in tightly stoppered bottles. Serve neat or mix with soda; or add a spoonful to a glass of white or sparkling wine.

COOK'S NOTE For a very smooth cordial, strain the blackberry purée through a piece of muslin, squeezing to extract all the juice.

GINGERADE

Thirst-quenching beverages were prepared in hot weather to take to the workers in the fields. Ginger was much used for spicing the drinks – in quantities that would probably not be palatable to us today.

4–6 SERVINGS

1½–2 tablespoons finely chopped fresh ginger
1½ teaspoons grated lemon zest
1.2 litres/2 pints boiling water
2 tablespoons freshly squeezed lemon juice
or more to taste
4 tablespoons mild liquid honey or more to taste

Put the ginger and lemon zest in a jug and pour in the boiling water. Stir, then leave to steep for about 1 hour.

Strain the liquid. Stir in the lemon juice and honey. Taste and add more lemon juice or honey if liked. Serve lightly chilled.

HERBADE

Shaker journals contain many recipes for delicious beverages, both hot and cold.

6 SERVINGS

100 g/3½ oz caster sugar
250 ml/8 fl oz water
30 g/1 oz fresh mint leaves, coarsely chopped
15 g/½ oz fresh lemon balm leaves, coarsely chopped
125 ml/4 fl oz freshly squeezed lemon juice
125 ml/4 fl oz freshly squeezed orange juice
1 litre/1⅔ pints chilled sparkling mineral water

Put the sugar and water in a saucepan and bring to the boil, stirring to dissolve the sugar. Boil the syrup for about 5 minutes. Leave to cool slightly.

Combine the herbs, sugar syrup and juices in a bowl and stir well to mix. Cover and leave to stand for at least 1 hour, mashing the herbs with a fork or spoon now and then.

Strain the mixture into a jug, pressing the herbs to extract all liquid. Just before serving, stir in the sparkling mineral water. Serve over ice.

COOK'S NOTE If you have no lemon balm growing in your garden, use 40 g/1½ oz mint (preferably different varieties) and add 1 tablespoon grated lemon zest.

OVERLEAF: LEFT TO RIGHT – GINGERADE, HERBADE,
RASPBERRY SHRUB

HANCOCK SHAKER VILLAGE, MASSACHUSETTS, WHICH HAS THE LARGEST COLLECTION OF SHAKER ARTEFACTS AND BUILDINGS

THE SHAKER COMMUNITIES

1787–1938 Watervliet (Niskeyuna), New York
4 Families, 2,668 members over 151 years

1787–1947 Mount (New) Lebanon, New York
8 Families, 3,202 members over 160 years; now a museum

1790–1960 Hancock, Massachusetts
6 Families, 548 members over 170 years; now a museum village

1790/2–1917 Enfield, Connecticut
5 Families, 739 members over 125 years

1792–1994 Canterbury, New Hampshire
3 Families, 746 members over 202 years; now a museum village

1792–1875 Tyringham, Massachusetts
2 Families, 241 members over 83 years

1793–1932 Alfred, Maine
3 Families, 241 members over 139 years

1793–1923 Enfield, New Hampshire
3 Families, 511 members over 130 years; now a museum

1793–1918 Harvard, Massachusetts
4 Families, 869 members over 125 years (with Shirley community)

1793–1908 Shirley, Massachusetts
3 Families

1794 Sabbathday Lake (New Gloucester), Maine
3 Families, 202 members over 200 years; still active

1806–1912 Union Village, Ohio
6 Families, 3,873 members over 106 years

1806–1910 Watervliet (Beulah), Ohio
2 Families, 127 members over 104 years

1806–1910 Pleasant Hill, Kentucky
numbers not known; now a museum village

1807/10–1922 South Union, Kentucky
4 Families, 676 members over 115 years; now a museum

1810/11–1827 West Union (Busro), Indiana
2 Families, numbers not known

1822–1889 North Union (Shaker Heights), Ohio
3 Families, 407 members over 67 years; now a museum

1824/5–1907 Whitewater, Ohio
3 Families, 491 members over 83 years

1826–1895 Sodus Bay and Groveland, New York
2 Families, 793 members over 69 years

SELECT BIBLIOGRAPHY

monthly periodicals of the society, first called *The Shaker* and later *Shaker and Shakeress*, *The Shaker Manifesto* and *The Manifesto*, New York and New Hampshire, 1871–1899.

Andrews, Edward Deming. *The Gift to be Simple: Songs, Dances and Rituals of the American Shakers,* New York, 1940.
———. *The People Called Shakers: The Search for a Perfect Society,* New York, 1953.
Andrews, Edward Deming and Faith Andrews. *Work and Worship Among the Shakers: Their Craftsmanship and Economic Order*, New York, 1982 (first published as *Work and Worship: The Economic Order of the Shakers,* Greenwich, Connecticut, 1974).
Brewer, Priscilla J. *Shaker Communities, Shaker Lives,* Hanover, New Hampshire, 1986.
Brown, Dale. *American Cooking,* New York, 1968.
Brown, Thomas. *An Account of the People Called Shakers, Their Faith, Doctrines, and Practice,* Troy, 1812.
Carr, Sister Frances A. *Shaker your Plate: of Shaker Cooks and Cooking*, Sabbathday Lake, Maine, 1985.
Dickens, Charles. *American Notes, written for General Circulation,* New York, first published 1842.
Druggist's Hand-book of Pure Botanic Preparations etc. sold by the Society of Shakers, Mount Lebanon, Columbia County, New York, 1873.
Dunlavy, John. *The Manifesto,* Pleasant Hill, Kentucky, 1847.
Extract from an unpublished manuscript on Shaker history (by an eye witness) giving an accurate description of their songs, dances, marches, visions, visits to the spirit land, etc., Boston, 1850.
Foster, Lawrence. *Women, Family and Utopia,* New York, 1991.
Haller, James with Jeffrey Paige. *Cooking in the Shaker Spirit,* Camden, Maine, 1990.
Horsham, Michael. *The Art of the Shakers,* New York, 1989.
Jones, Evan. *American Food: The Gastronomic Story,* New York, 1974.
Kitch, Sally L. *Chaste Liberation: Celibacy and Female Cultural Status,* University of Illinois Press, 1989.
Kremer, Elizabeth C. *We Make You Kindly Welcome:*

Recipes from the Trustees' House Daily Fare, Harrodsburg, Kentucky, 1970.
———. *Welcome Back to Pleasant Hill: More Recipes from the Trustees' House,* Harrodsburg, Kentucky, 1977.
Lindsay, Eldress Bertha. *Seasoned with Grace,* Canterbury, New Hampshire, 1987.
Melcher, Marguerite F. *The Shaker Adventure,* Princeton, New Jersey, 1941.
Miller, Amy Bess. *Shaker Herbs,* New York, 1976.
Miller, Amy Bess and Persis Fuller. *The Best of Shaker Cooking,* New York, 1985.
Monroe, Candace Ord. *Shaker Style,* New York, 1991.
Neal, Julia. *The Kentucky Shakers,* University Press of Kentucky, 1977.
Nordhoff, Charles. *The Communistic Societies of the United States from Personal Visits and Observation,* New York, 1875.
Paige, Jeffrey S. *The Shaker Kitchen,* New York, 1994.
Peculiarities of the Shakers described in a series of letters from Lebanon Springs, in the year 1832, containing an account of the origin, worship, and doctrines of the Shakers' Society by a visiter
Piercy, Caroline B. with Arthur Tolve. *The Shaker Cookbook: Recipes and Lore from The Valley of God's Pleasure,* Bowling Green, Ohio, 1984 (previously published as *The Shaker Cookbook: Not by Bread Alone,* New York, 1953)
Sears, Clara Endicott. *Gleanings from Old Shaker Journals,* Boston and New York, 1916.
Sprigg, June. *By Shaker Hands,* University Press of New England, 1975.
Sprigg, June with David Larkin. *Shaker Life, Work and Art,* New York, 1987.
Stein, Stephen J. *The Shaker Experience in America,* Yale University Press, 1992.
Wells, Seth and Calvin Green."The Shakers," *Cyclopedia of Religious Denominations containing authentic accounts of the different creeds and systems prevailing throughout the world,* London, 1853.
Wertkin, Gerard C. *The Four Seasons of Shaker Life,* New York, 1986.
White, Anna and Leila Taylor. *Shakerism: Its Meaning and Message,* Columbus, Ohio, 1905.

RECIPE INDEX

LIST OF RECIPES

SOUPS

Spring vegetable and herb soup
Fresh sweetcorn chowder
Spicy baked bean soup
Potato and leek soup
Cream of squash soup
Beef and vegetable soup
Old-fashioned chicken soup with noodles
Fish chowder
Oyster stew

FISH, POULTRY AND MEAT

Fish and eggs
Codfish balls
Boiled fish with a rich sauce
Baked fish with herb stuffing
Fried chicken with cream gravy
Chestnut and herb stuffing for turkey
Chicken breasts with fried apples
Chicken potpie
Hot turkey or chicken and mushroom sandwiches
Meat loaf
Beef stew with herb dumplings
Pot roast with horseradish sauce
Pork chops in soured cream
Lamb and barley stew
Lamb steaks with herb butter
Lamb knuckles with dried fruit

Ham baked in cider
Bacon and egg hand pies
Ham and potato hash

VEGETARIAN DISHES

Lentil loaf
Vegetable potpie
Asparagus and Cheddar pudding
Tomato cream pie
Smothered onion pie
Fluffy cheese and chive omelette
Spinach custard with tomato sauce
Mushroom and rice cakes
Baked stuffed acorn squash
Fried cornmeal mush with courgettes

SIDE DISHES

Creamed potatoes
Fried tomatoes
Baked squash
Cucumbers in cream
Glazed carrots
Green beans with bacon
Potato cakes with rosemary
Beetroot in honey
Slow-baked beans

Green corn fritters
Home-made noodles
Cabbage salad
Green bean salad
Cucumber and mint salad

BREADS AND BAKING

Maple wheaten bread
Sweet potato bread
Scented leaf rolls
Herb and cheese bread
Corn bread
Steamed brown bread
Whipped cream biscuits
Rosewater sponge cake
Mother Ann's birthday cake
Gingerbread
Spicy applesauce cake
Comb honey cake
Fruit and nut loaf
Pecan muffins
Sugar cookies
Cinnamon soured cream cookies
Pecan balls
Molasses cookies
Cranberry oat cookies

DESSERTS, PIES AND CANDIES

Apple and blackberry batter pudding
Baked rice pudding

Bread pudding
Blueberry crisp
Citrus sponge pudding with cherry sauce
Strawberry shortcake
Apple dumplings
Summer berry pudding
Baked peaches
Iced lemon cream
Berry water ice
Rosewater ice cream
Rhubarb and strawberry pie
Apple pie
Lemon pie
Peach and apricot leather
Maple pecan fudge
Molasses cream taffy

PRESERVES, SAUCES AND BEVERAGES

Sweetcorn relish
Cranberry catsup
Spiced pickled pears
Boiled cider syrup
Herb vinegars
Apple butter
Applesauce
Raspberry shrub
Blackberry cordial
Gingerade
Herbade

PICTURE ACKNOWLEDGMENTS

With grateful thanks to the following individuals and organizations
who helped make this book possible:

Canterbury Shaker Village, New Hampshire: pages 11, 17, 74, 131

Fruitlands Museum, Harvard, Massachusetts: page 8

Hancock Shaker Village, Pittsfield, Massachusetts: pages 23, 29

Tim Lamb, James Merrell and Nadia McKenzie for Shaker Ltd:
pages 15, 18, 20, 21, 22, 27, 69, 73, 103, 109, 112, 121, 138

Shaker Museum, Old Chatham, New York: page 139

The Shaker Shops, 25 Harcourt Street, London W1, and 322 King's
Road, London SW3. (Tel: 0171 724 7672.)
Shaker in London strives to emulate the commercial values of
traditional Shaker. It employs cratsmen in America and Britain who
have specialist skills in reproducing Shaker products such as oval
boxes and baskets. The suppliers, cabinet makers and tinsmiths use
the finest materials and traditional methods to create exclusive
products. The majority of the furniture is produced by Shaker
Workshops in Massachusetts, and The Shakers at Sabbathday Lake
supply the teas and herbs sold in the shop.

Philip Webb: all food and ingredients photography and styling